D1375566

THIS IS A CARLTON BOOK

Text copyright © Hatchette Emap Magazines Limited, 2000, 2001 and 2003
Design and artwork copyright © Carlton Publishing Group, 2000, 2001 and 2003

This edition published in 2004 by Carlton Books Ltd
A Division of the Carlton Publishing Group
20 Mortimer Street
London
W1T 3JW

This book is sold subject to the condition that it shall not, by way of trade or otherwise,
be lent, resold, hired out or otherwise circulated without the publisher's prior written
consent in any form of cover or binding other than that in which it is published and
without a similar condition including this condition, being imposed upon the
subsequent purchaser.

All rights reserved.

A CIP catalogue for this book is available from the British Library.

ISBN 1 84442 664 5

Editorial Manager: Venetia Penfold
Senior Art Editors: Diane Spender and Barbara Zuñiga
Editor: Louise Johnson
Production: Garry Lewis
Illustrations: Sarah Nayler

CARLTON BOOKS

NEWwoman

Edited by **Louise Johnson**

the BIGGEST

book of

Bloke Jokes

Ever

...because men just get
funnier and funnier

CONTENTS

1

GREAT MYSTERIES OF OUR TIME (I) –

WHAT'S ALL THAT ABOUT?

What do you give **the bloke** who has everything?

Penicillin.

What happens when a bloke eats a mosquito?

He has more brain cells in his stomach than his head.

What do you get when you offer a bloke a penny for his thoughts?

Change.

What's the thickest **book** in the world?

What Blokes Think They Know About Women.

What do you get when four **blokes** go fishing together and one comes back after catching nothing?

Three Men And A Baby.

What do you see when you look into a bloke's eyes?

The back of his head.

What is the proof that the average woman can take a joke?

The average bloke.

What do you do with a bloke who thinks he's God's gift to women?

Take him back and exchange him.

What happens when a woman makes a fool of a bloke?

It's usually an improvement.

What happened when the woman put an ad in the classifieds saying 'Husband wanted'?

Next day she received a hundred letters all saying: 'You can have mine.'

What's the best revenge when a woman steals your bloke?

Let her keep him.

What's the definition of a wedding tragedy?

Marrying a bloke for love, and then finding out he has no money.

What do you never **want to hear while having great sex?**

Honey, I'm home!

What do you call an attractive, intelligent and sensitive man?

A rumour.

What's the difference between a man and a yoghurt?

A yoghurt has culture!

What's the difference between Bigfoot and an intelligent bloke?

Bigfoot's been spotted
several times.

What do most blokes consider a gourmet restaurant?

Any place without a
drive-up window.

What's the best place to hide a bloke's birthday present?

The washing basket.

What's the difference between a bloke with a mid-life crisis and a clown?

A clown knows he's
wearing funny clothes.

What's easier to make, a snowman or a snowwoman?

A snowwoman – because with
a snowman you have to hollow
out the head and use all that extra
snow to make its *testicles*.

What's the difference between a bloke and Bigfoot?

One is covered with
matted hair and *smells awful*.
The other has big feet.

What's a bloke's idea of helping to make the bed?

Getting out of it.

What's a bloke's definition of 'conflict of interest'?

When pizza
arrives during sex.

What's a bloke's idea of helping around the house?

Dropping his
clothes where you
can pick them up.

What's a bloke's definition of recycling?

Using beer cans as ashtrays before throwing them on the side of the road.

2

EVERYONE LIKES A LIST, DON'T THEY? (I)

How to Tell Someone Their Fly Is Unzipped...

- You've got your fly set for 'Monica' instead of 'Hillary.'

- You've got Windows on your laptop.

- Quasimodo needs to go back in the tower and tend to his bells.

- Paging Mr. Johnson... Paging Mr. Johnson...

- Your pod bay door is open, Hal.

- Elvis Junior has left the building!

- Mini Me is making a break for fame.

- Ensign Hanes is reporting a hull breach on the lower deck, Sir!

- Captain, sensors detect a wormhole in the forward quadrant!

- Sailor Ned's trying to take a little shore leave.

- Your dork is ajar.

- You've got a security breach at Los Pantalones.

- I see you have an opening in senior management.

- Our next guest is someone who needs no introduction.

— Hi ya!

The Eight Qualities
Of A Perfect Husband

- **B**rave
- **I**ntelligent
- **G**entle
- **P**olite
- **E**nergetic
- **N**utty
- **I**ndustrious
- **S**ensitive

**And if all else fails, well...
read the CAPITAL LETTERS only**

New chemical element

Element name: Man

Symbol: XY **Atomic weight**: (180 +/-50)

Physical properties: Solid at room temperature, but gets bent out of shape easily. Fairly dense and sometimes flaky. Difficult to find a pure sample. Due to rust, ageing samples are unable to conduct electricity as easily as young samples.

Chemical properties: Attempts to bond with WO (Element: woman) any chance it can get. Also tends to form strong bonds with itself. Becomes explosive when mixed with KD (Element: child) for prolonged period of time. Neutralise by saturating with alcohol.

Usage: None known. Possibly good source of methane. Good specimens are able to produce large quantities on command.

Caution: In the absence of WO, this element rapidly decomposes and begins to smell.

Evening classes for blokes

- The Gas Gauge In Your Car: Sometimes Empty **MEANS** Empty.

- Dressing Up: Beyond the Funeral and the Wedding

- Going To The Supermarket: It's Not Just For Women Anymore!

- Giving Back To The Community: How To Donate 15-Year-Old Levis To Oxfam.

- Romance: More Than A Cable Channel!

- Directions: It's Okay To Ask for Them.

- Strange But True: She Really May NOT Care What The Offside Trap Is About.

- 'I Could Have Played a Better Game Than That!': Why Women Laugh.

- 'I Don't Know': Be The First Bloke To Say It!

Put downs for blokes who really deserve them:

- ### Are those your eyeballs? I found them in my cleavage.

- Did the aliens forget to remove your anal probe?

- Whatever kind of look you were going for, you missed.

- It ain't the size, it's... no, it's the size.

- I'm trying to imagine you with a personality.

- Too many freaks, not enough circuses.

- Nice aftershave. Must you marinate in it?

- And which dwarf are you?

- If I want to hear the pitter patter of little feet, I'll put shoes on my cats.

- Did I mention the kick in the groin you'll be receiving if you touch me?

Condom mania

Imagine if all major retailers started making their own condoms and keeping the same tagline...

Polo condoms – the condom with the hole!!! (VERY poor seller!!!).

Sainsbury's Condoms – making life taste better.

Abbey National condoms – because life is complicated enough.

Pringles condoms – once you pop, you can't stop.

Burger King condoms – Home of the whopper.

Goodyear condoms – 'for a longer ride go wide.'

Renault condoms – size really does matter!

Domestos condoms – get right under the rim!

Why are blokes just dogs without the fur?

- They spend all day sprawled on the most comfortable piece of furniture in the house.

- They can hear food opening half a mile away, but don't hear you when you're in the same room.

- They can look dumb and lovable all at the same time.

- They growl when they're not happy.

- When you want to play, they want to play.

- When you want to be alone, they want to play.

- They leave their toys everywhere.

- They do disgusting things with their mouths and then try to give you a kiss!

- They go right to your crotch as soon as they meet you.

Blokespeak (phrasebook for the opposite sex)

- 'Haven't I seen you before?'   *translation*   **'Nice ass.'**

- 'I'm a Romantic.'   *translation*   **'I'm poor'**

- 'I need you'   *translation*   **'My hand is tired'**

Five secrets of a perfect relationship

1 It is important to find a man who
helps at home, who cooks from time
to time, who cleans up and who has a job.

2 It is important to find a man
who can ***make you laugh***.

3 It is important to find a man who you
can trust and who ***doesn't lie*** to you.

4 It is important to find a man who is
good in bed and who likes to be with you.

*****

5 It is very important that these
four men ***don't know each other***.

Things that are difficult for blokes to say when they're drunk:

- Innovative.

- Preliminary.

- Proliferation.

- Cinnamon.

Things that are VERY difficult for blokes to say when they're drunk:

- Specificity.

- British Constitution.

- Passive-aggressive disorder.

- Transubstantiate.

Things that are Downright Impossible for blokes to say when they're drunk:

- Thanks, but I don't want to sleep with you.

- Nope, no more booze for me.

- Sorry, but you're not really my type.

- No kebab for me, thank you.

- Good evening officer, isn't it a lovely evening.

- Oh, I just couldn't – no-one wants to hear me sing.

- No, I won't make any attempt to dance thanks, I have zero coordination.

A two-year degree is being offered at Life University that many of you should be interested in: **Becoming A Real Bloke**. That's right, in just six terms, you, too, can be a real bloke.

Please take a moment to look over the program outline.

FIRST YEAR

Autumn Term:

- MEN 101 Combating Stupidity

- MEN 102 You, Too, Can Do Housework

- MEN 103 PMS – Learn When To Keep Your Mouth Shut

- MEN 104 We Do Not Want Sleazy Underthings For Christmas

Winter Term:

- MEN 110 Wonderful Laundry Techniques

- MEN 111 Understanding The Female Response To Getting In At 4am

- MEN 112 Parenting: It Doesn't End With Conception

- EAT 100 Get A Life, Learn To Cook

- EAT 101 Get A Life, Learn To Cook II

- ECON 001A What's Hers Is Hers

Spring Term:

- MEN 120 How NOT To Act Like An Arse When You're Wrong

- MEN 121 Understanding Your Incompetence

- MEN 122 YOU, The Weaker Sex

- MEN 123 Reasons To Give Flowers

SECOND YEAR

Autumn Term:

- SEX 101 You CAN Fall Asleep Without It

- SEX 102 Morning Dilemma: If It's Awake, Take A Shower

- MEN 201 How To Stay Awake After Sex

- MEN 202 How To Put the Toilet Seat Down – Optional
  (See other options below)

Winter Term:

- MEN 210 The Remote Control: Overcoming Your Dependency

- MEN 211 How To Not Act Younger Than Your Children

- MEN 212 You, Too, Can Be A Designated Driver

- MEN 213 Honest, You Don't Look Like Tom Cruise,
  Especially When Naked

- MEN 230A Her Birthdays And Anniversaries Are Important

Spring Term:

- MEN 220 Omitting %&*! From Your Vocabulary (Pass/Fail Only)

- MEN 221 Fluffing The Blanket After Farting Is Not Necessary

- MEN 222 Real Blokes Ask For Directions

- MEN 223 Thirty Minutes Of Begging Is NOT Considered Foreplay

- MEN 230B Her Birthdays And Anniversaries Are Important II

Course Options:

- EAT 101 Cooking With Tofu

- EAT 102 Utilisation Of Eating Utensils

- EAT 103 Burping And Belching Discreetly

- MEN 231 Mothers-in-law

- MEN 232 Appear To Be Listening

- MEN 233 Just Say 'Yes, Dear'

- ECON 001B Cheaper To Keep Her (Must Pass ECON 001A)

3

DOCTOR, DOCTOR...(1)

Did you hear about the bloke who mistook Viagra for his sleeping tablets?

He woke up with a stiff neck.

An 88-year-old woman goes to the doctor for Viagra for her **90-year-old** husband. The bemused doctor asks whether she wants regular, strong or extra potent tablets. When she replied 'regular' the doctor queried her choice because of her husband's advanced age, suggesting that **'extra strong'** might be more suitable. 'Oh, it's not for that,' the wife replied, a little embarrassed. 'I just want him to stop **peeing on his feet**!'

A bloke returns from the doctor and tells his wife that he's been given just **24 hours to live**. Given this prognosis, he asks his wife for sex. Naturally, she agrees, and they make love.

About six hours later, the bloke goes to his wife and says, 'Honey, you know I now have only **18 hours to live**. Could we please do it one more time?'

Of course, the wife agrees and they do it again. Later, as the bloke gets into bed, he looks at his watch and realises that he now has only 8 hours left.

He touches his wife's shoulder and asks, 'Honey, please... just one more time before I die.' She says, 'Of course, dear.' And they **make love for the third time**. After this session, the wife rolls over and falls asleep.

The bloke, however, worried about his impending death, tosses and turns until he's down to **4 more hours**. He taps his wife, who rouses. 'Honey, I have only 4 more hours. Do you think we could...'

At this point the wife sits up and says, 'Listen honey, I have to get up in the morning, **you don't**.'

A bloke with a winking problem is applying for a position as a sales representative for a large firm. The interviewer is bowled over: 'This is phenomenal. You've graduated from the best schools; your recommendations are wonderful and your experience is unparalleled. Normally, we'd hire you without a second thought, but we're afraid your constant winking might scare off potential customers.' 'Wait,' says the bloke. 'If I take two aspirin, I'll stop winking!' He reaches into his jacket pocket and begins pulling out all sorts of **condoms**: red, blue, ribbed, flavoured; finally, at the bottom, he finds a packet of aspirin and after swallowing two he stops winking in a few moments. 'That's all well and good,' says the interviewer. 'But this is a respectable company, we can't have our **employees womanising** all over the country!'

'What do you mean?' says the bloke. 'I'm a happily married man!'

'So how do you **explain all these condoms?**'

'Oh, that,' he sighed. 'Have you ever walked into a pharmacy, **winking**, and asked for aspirin?'

An eighty-year-old bloke was having an annual **physical**. As the doctor was listening to his heart with the stethoscope, he began muttering, 'Oh oh!'

The bloke asked the doctor what the problem was.

'Well,' said the doc, 'You have a serious heart murmur. Do you smoke?'

'No,' replied the bloke.

'Do you **drink in excess**?'

'No,' replied the bloke.

'Do you have a **sex life**?'

'Yes, I do!'

'Well,' said the doc, 'I'm afraid with this heart murmur, you'll have to **give up half your sex life**.'

Looking perplexed, the old bloke said, 'Which half – the looking or the thinking?'

And what about the new **Viagra** eyedrops? They're not much good for your eyes, they just make blokes look **hard**.

A bloke goes to the doctor with a piece of lettuce **sticking out of his bum**. He tells the doctor he's a little concerned, and asks for an examination.

After a **little probing**, the doctor turns to his patient and says 'It's worse than I originally thought – that's just the tip of the iceberg.'

Blokes beware – it's been revealed that criminals who steal Viagra will face **stiff** sentencing.

A bloke goes to the doctors and says: 'Doctor, every time I sneeze **I have an orgasm**.'

The doctor says: 'What are you taking for it?'

And the bloke replies: **'Pepper!'**

There's a new drink on the market today. It is called Viagraccino – one cup and you're up all night.

A bloke is in a terrible accident, and his '**manhood**' is mangled and torn from his body. His doctor assures him that modern medicine could replace it but that his insurance wouldn't cover the surgery, since it was considered cosmetic. The doctor gives him three quotes: £3,500 for **small**, £6,500 for **medium**, and £14,000 for **large**. The bloke was pretty sure he wanted a large, but the doctor urged him to talk it over with his wife before he made any decision. So the bloke leaves the room to call his wife to explain their options, but returns looking very dejected. 'Well, what have the two of you decided?' asks the doctor. The bloke answers: 'She'd rather have a new kitchen.'

Doctor, you've got to help me,'
says the bloke on the couch.
'Every night I have the same
horrible dream. I'm lying in bed
when all of a sudden five women
rush in and start tearing off my
clothes.'

The psychiatrist nods. 'And what do
you do when this happens?'

'I push them away,' says the bloke.

'I, see,' replies the psychiatrist. 'And
what do you want me to do?'

'Break my arms!'

This bloke's been having a few '**arousal**' **problems** and goes to see a **private doctor** who prescribes **Viagra**. Armed with the prescription he goes with his wife to the chemist and is shocked to find that the price is £10 per pill. 'Oh well,' says his wife. '£40 a year isn't too bad!'

A bloke goes to see his doctor for his test results, and things are looking really grim. 'I'm sorry,' says the doctor, 'but you only have three minutes to live.'

'Surely there must be something you can do for me?' begs the bloke.

'Well,' says the doctor. **'I could boil you an egg...'**

4

GREAT MYSTERIES OF OUR TIME (II) – HOW COME?

How do you make 7 pounds of fat look attractive to a bloke?

Put a nipple on it.

How do most blokes define marriage?

A very expensive way of getting their laundry done free.

How do blokes know when the clocks have gone back?

When their 5 o'clock shadow appears at 4 o'clock.

How do you make a bloke's eyes light up?

Shine a torch in his ear.

How does a man show that he is planning for the future?

He buys **two** cases of beer.

**How do you tell if your
bloke's died during sex?**

He stays **stiff** for longer
than two minutes.

**How can you tell if a bloke has a small
penis, without touching or looking?**

Check out the sports
car in his driveway.

How stupid are blokes about money?

Only a man would
buy a £500 car and put
a £4,000 stereo in it.

**How can you tell that
soap operas are fictional?**

In real life, blokes aren't affectionate in bed.

**How is being at a singles bar
different to being at the circus?**

At the circus, the clowns don't talk.

How do blokes' braincells die?

Alone.

How do blokes define
a '50/50' relationship?

We cook – they eat; we clean –
they dirty; we iron – they wrinkle.

How many blokes does
it take to change a light bulb?

Four – one to carry the tool box,
one to wear the utility belt, one to read
the DIY manual and one to do the job.

How do you know when it's time
to wash dishes and clean the house?

Look inside your pants;
if you have a penis, it's **not** time.

How do you scare blokes?

Sneak up
behind them
and start
throwing confetti.

How do you know when a bloke wants sex?

He's awake!

How do crazy blokes walk through the forest?

They take the psycho path.

How many blokes does it take to change a lightbulb?

Five. One to actually change the lightbulb and the rest to join him down the pub afterwards to moan about what a busy day he'd had!

How do you get a bloke to lift a feather duster?

Put it on top of the remote control!

How do blokes practise safe sex?

They meet their mistresses at least 50 miles from home.

How many blokes does it take to change a lightbulb?

At least two – one to climb the ladder and the other to tell him why he's doing it wrong!

**How can you make sure
your bloke doesn't make
a fool of himself at a party?**

Leave him at home.

**How do you keep a bloke
interested after marriage?**

Wear perfume that
smells like beer.

How can you tell that women have a sense of humour?

They get married.

5

SO THIS BLOKE GOES INTO A PUB...(I)

This bloke walks into a bar on the top of a very tall building. He sits down, orders a huge beer, downs it in one, walks over to the window, and **jumps out**. Five minutes later, he walks back into the bar, orders another huge beer, downs it in one, walks over to the window, and **jumps out again**. Five minutes later, he comes back and does the whole thing again. Not being able to contain his curiosity, another bloke at the bar stops him and says, 'I've got to ask how on earth are you doing that?!' The first bloke responds, 'Oh, it's simple physics, really. When you down the beer in one, it makes you all warm inside and since warm air rises, if you just hold your breath you become lighter than air and float down to the pavement.' '**Wow!**' exclaims the second bloke, '**I've got to have a go**'. So he orders a huge beer, downs it in one, goes over to the window, **jumps out**, and splats on the pavement below. The barman looks over to the first bloke and says, 'Superman, you're a **tosser** when you're drunk!'

This bloke goes into a pub followed by an **ostrich**. They both sit down and order two beers. Then the bloke reaches in his pocket and pulls out the exact money for the beers. Over the next few weeks they become regulars at the pub, always ordering drinks and paying with the correct change. The barman finally asks the bloke, 'How come you always have the right change?' The bloke replies: 'I found one of those magic genie bottles on the beach one day and made a couple of wishes. The first one was that I would always have the right amount of money to pay for anything I wanted.'

'That's ingenious,' says the barman. 'But what's with the ostrich?' 'Well,' says the bloke. 'I also wished for a **chick with long legs**.'

SO THIS BLOKE GOES INTO A PUB...(1)

Two blokes are sitting at the bar and one says, 'I remember the first time I used alcohol as a substitute for women.' 'Yeah, what happened?' asked the other bloke. The first bloke replies: 'I got my **knob stuck** in the neck of the bottle.'

This bloke's sitting in a pub, just looking at his drink. He stays like that for half-an-hour. Then a big tough-looking truck driver walks up to him, takes the drink, and swallows it all. The poor bloke starts crying.

The truck driver says: 'Come on, I was just joking. Here, I'll buy you another drink. I can't see a bloke crying.'

'No, it's not that,' says the bloke. 'This day is the worst of my life.

First, I overslept, and got to work late. My boss was furious, so fired me. When I left the building to go to my car, I found out it was stolen. Then the police said they couldn't do anything. I got a taxi home, and when I left the cab, I realised I'd left my wallet and credit cards in it. I got indoors and I found my wife in bed with the gardener. So I left home to come to this pub.

And just as I was thinking about putting an end to my life, you show up and drink my poison...'

A **bloke** walks into a pub and says, 'Give me two whiskies. One for me and one for my best mate.' The barman says, 'You want them both now or do you want me to wait until your mate arrives to pour his?' The bloke says, 'Oh, I want them both now. I've got my best mate in my pocket here.' He then pulls a little three inch man out of his pocket. The barman is amazed: 'Are you sure he can drink that much?' 'Of course,' says the bloke, you just watch. And with that the little man drank his whisky. 'What else can he do? Can he walk?' asks the barman. The man flicks a pound coin down to the end of the bar and says, 'Go on Bob, go and get the money.' The little man runs down to the end of the bar, picks up the pound coin, runs back down and gives it to the bloke. The barman's in total shock. 'That's amazing!' he says. 'What else can he do? Does he talk?' The bloke looks up at the bartender with a look of surprise in his eye and says: 'Talk? Sure he talks. Oi, Bob, tell him about that time we were in Africa on safari and you called that native Witch doctor an **asshole**!'

Two blokes are sitting in a pub and one is getting really depressed about the fact that his wife has left him. He keeps insisting that he's useless, but after a few pints his mate has convinced him he's better off without her. Then all of a sudden the dumped bloke bursts into tears. 'I don't even know what setting to use on the washing machine!' 'Oh, that's simple,' says the other bloke. 'What does it say on your shirt?'

'Arsenal.'

A couple are sitting in a bar when the bloke notices an advert for alcopops showing a bare-chested hunk complete with six pack. 'Yeah, right,' says the bloke sarcastically. 'So if I drink ten bottles of that I'll look like him, will I?' 'No,' replies his girlfriend. 'When **I** drink ten bottles of that, **you'll** look like him!'

A bloke walks into a pub and asks the landlady for a double entendre. So she gives him one.

Two blokes go to the pub for their lunch. One of the blokes calls the waitress over and asks her for a quickie. Not surprisingly she slaps his face and storms off. Then his mate says to him: 'It's pronounced "quiche".'

6

IT'S A
BIBLE
THING (I)!

An old bloke goes into a Catholic Church and sits down in the confessional booth:

Bloke: 'I am 92 years old, have a wonderful wife of 70 years, many children, grandchildren, and great grandchildren. But yesterday I picked up two students who were hitchhiking. We went to a hotel, and I had sex with them three times.'

Priest: 'Are you sorry for your **sins?**'

Bloke: 'What **sins?**'

Priest: 'What kind of Catholic are you?'

Bloke: 'I'm not Catholic!'

Priest: 'Then why are you telling me all this?'

Bloke: 'I'm telling absolutely **everyone**!'

The **TRUE** story of creation...

In The Beginning, God created the **Heaven and the Earth.** And the Earth was without form, and void, and darkness was upon the face of the deep.

And the Devil said, 'It doesn't get any better than this.'

And so **God created Man** in His own image;

Male and female He created them.

And God looked upon **Man** and **Woman**

And saw that they were **lean and fit**.

And God **populated** the earth

With **broccoli** and **cauliflower** and **spinach**

And **green** and **yellow vegetables** of all kinds,

So **Man** and **Woman** would live long and **healthy** lives.

And so the Devil created **Fast Food Giants**.

And Fast Food Giants brought forth the **99p double cheeseburger**.

And the Devil said to Man, '**You want fries with that?**'

And Man said, '**Super-size them**.'

And Man **gained five pounds**.

And God said, '**Why** doth thou eatest thus?'

I have sent the **heart-healthy vegetables**

And **olive oil** with which to cook them.'

But the Devil brought forth **chicken fried steak**

So big it needed its own platter.

And Man gained **10 pounds**

And his **cholesterol** went through the roof.

And so God brought forth **running shoes**.

And Man resolved to lose **those extra pounds**.

And the Devil brought forth **cable TV** with **remote control**

So Man would not have to toil to **change channels** between **Sky Sports 1** and **Sky Sports 2**.

And Man gained another **20 pounds**.

And so God brought forth the **potato**,

A vegetable naturally low in fat and brimming with nutrition.

And the Devil peeled off the **healthful skin** and sliced the starchy centre into **chips** and deep-fat fried them.

And the Devil created **sour cream** dip.

And Man clutched his **remote control**

And ate the potato chips swaddled in **cholesterol**.

And the Devil saw and said, '**It is good**.'

And Man went into **cardiac arrest**.

And God sighed and created **quadruple bypass** surgery.

And the Devil cancelled Man's **health insurance**.

So God showed **Woman** how to peel the skin off chicken

And cook the nourishing **whole grain brown rice**.

And the Devil created **light beer**

So Man could **poison his body**,

While feeling righteous because he had to **drink twice as much** of the now-insipid brew to get the same buzz.

And Man gained another **10 pounds**.

And **Woman** ventured forth

Into the land of **chocolates**,
And upon returning asked Man, **'Do I look fat?'**
And the Devil said, **'Always tell the truth.'**
And **Man did**.
And Woman went out from the presence of Man
And dwelt in the land of the **divorce lawyer**,
East of the marriage counsellor.
And the Devil said, '**It really doesn't get any better than this**.'

The three wise men arrived to visit the child lying in the manger. One of the wise men was exceptionally tall and bumped his head on the low doorway as he entered the stable. 'Jesus Christ!' he exclaimed.

Joseph said: 'Write that down, Mary; it's better than Clyde!'

Why did God make blokes first?

She wanted to start with something simple.

Dopey and the other seven dwarves are meeting the Pope at the Vatican. Dopey sidles up to him and says, 'Excuse me, Your Holiness, but **are there any dwarf nuns in Rome?**' The Pope thinks about it and says, 'No, Dopey, I don't think there are.'

Dopey shuffles from one foot to the other. '**Are there any dwarf nuns in the whole of Europe?**' Again, the Pope shakes his head.

Desperately now, Dopey says, '**Are there any dwarf nuns in the whole of the world?**' 'I'm sorry Dopey, but the answer is still no,' says the Pope. 'Why are you so concerned about this issue anyway?'

Shamefaced, Dopey points to the other six dwarves who are huddled in a corner, splitting their sides with laughter and chanting, '**Dopey shagged a penguin!**

A boat is slowly sinking and there's just one bloke left on board, praying. A lifeboat comes past and beckons him to jump on. 'No,' says the bloke. 'I have faith in the Lord. **God will save me**.'

The passenger continues to pray and suddenly a helicopter appears and throws down a rope. The pilot begs him to grab the rope but the bloke says: 'No, I have faith in the Lord. **God will save me**.' The boat continues to sink and the bloke continues to pray. Then a speedboat arrives, just as the boat is about to go down. But the bloke won't jump in and save himself. 'I have faith in the Lord,' he says. '**God will save me**.' Eventually the boat sinks and the bloke drowns. When he arrives in heaven he says to God: 'Lord, I trusted you all my life, but you let me down. I can't believe it.'

'You can't believe it!?' says God. '**And I sent you two bloody boats and a chopper!**'

7

SAY WHAT?

Bloke says: 'It's just **too hot** to wear clothes today, what do you reckon the neighbours would think if I mowed the lawn naked?'

huh?

New woman replies: 'Probably that I married you for your money.'

Bloke says: 'Shall we try swapping positions tonight?'

New woman replies: That's a good idea… you stand by the ironing board while I sit on the sofa and **burp**.'

Bloke says: 'This coffee isn't fit for a pig!'
New Woman replies: 'No problem. I'll get you some that is!'

Bloke says: 'When did you first realize you loved me?'
New woman replies: 'When I got upset at people saying you were ugly, fat and bloody useless!'

Bloke says:
'You know, I was
a fool when I married you.'
New woman replies:
'Yes, dear, but I
was in love and
didn't notice.'

Bloke says:
'Tonight I'm going
to make you the happiest
woman in the world.'
New woman replies:
'I'll miss you.'

Bloke says:
'Since I first
laid eyes on you,
I've wanted to make
love to you really badly.'
New woman replies:
'Well – you succeeded.'

Bloke says:
'Two inches more
and I'd be king!'
New woman replies:
'Two inches less,
and you'd be queen!'

Bloke says:
'Hey babe,
I'd sure love to get
into your pants.'
New woman replies:
'No thanks, I've already
got one arse in there.'

Bloke says:
'Will you tell me the
moment you orgasm?'
New woman replies:
'Only if you telephone!'

Bloke says:
'Haven't I seen you
someplace before?'
New woman replies:
'Yes, that's why I
don't go there anymore.'

Bloke says:
'Is this seat empty?'
New woman replies:
'Yes, and this one will
be if you sit down.'

Bloke says:
'Your place or mine?'
New woman replies:
'Both. You go to yours,
and I'll go to mine.'

Bloke says:
'Hey baby,
what's your sign?'
New woman replies:
'Do not enter.'

Bloke says:
'I'd go to the end of
the world for you.'
New woman replies:
'But would you
stay there?'

Bloke says:
'If I could see you
naked, I'd die happy.'
New woman replies:
'If I saw you naked,
I'd probably die laughing.'

Bloke says:
'Is there somebody else?'
New woman replies:
'Of course not.
Do you think I'd be
going out with an arse
like you if there was?'

8

WOMEN
ON TOP (I)

A bloke left work one Friday afternoon, but being pay-day, instead of going home, he stayed out the entire weekend **partying with the boys** and spending his entire wage packet.

When he finally appeared at home on Sunday night, he was confronted by a **very angry wife** and was shouted at for nearly two hours about what a **rubbish husband** he was. Finally his wife stopped the **nagging** and simply said to him. 'How would you like it if you didn't see me for two or three days?'

'That would be fine with me,' said the bloke.

* * *

Monday went by and he didn't see his wife. Tuesday and Wednesday came and went with the same results. But on Thursday, the **swelling went down** just enough so he could see her a little out of the corner of his left eye.

A bloke is sitting next to a woman on the plane. To try to get her talking he asks if she'll play a game with him. She refuses, so he tries again. 'What if I ask you a question and if you get it wrong **you pay me a fiver**, then you ask me a question and if I get it wrong I pay you £50?' She agrees, as long as she can go first, then says '**What goes up a hill red and comes down it blue?**' And with that she turns over to sleep. The bloke looks puzzled and spends three hours searching the Web on his laptop for the answer. Eventually he wakes her with the £50 and admits defeat.Well, what is it?' With that she takes a fiver from her purse, gives it to the bloke and **goes back to sleep**.

A bloke is standing in the garden watching his wife cooking **burgers on the barbeque**. 'You know dear,' he says. '**Your bum is almost as wide as the grill** now!' She just pretends she can't hear him. Later in bed that night he tries to get a little friendly with her but **she pushes him away**. 'Darling, what's the matter, don't you want me?' the bloke says. 'No,' she replies 'I don't really think it's worth heating up this big grill for just **half a sausage** is it?!'

A **very attractive blonde** woman walks into a casino and says to the dealers: 'I want to bet everything I have on one throw of the dice, but in order to be lucky I have to **take off all my clothes**.' The dealers look at each other, **can't believe their luck** and agree that this will be fine. The **woman strips off** all her clothes, rolls the dice and then starts jumping up and down screaming '**Yes! I've Won!**', scoops up a huge pile of chips and her discarded clothes and leaves the casino. After a pause, one dealer turns to the other and says, 'So what did she throw?' The second dealer shrugs, 'I have no idea, I thought you were watching the dice'.

Moral: Blondes are not always stupid, but blokes are always blokes!

Did you hear about the woman who finally figured blokes out?
She **died laughing** before she could tell anybody.

A bloke went home to his wife with a present in his hand, but when she opened it, there was just a **tube of KY jelly**. 'That will **make you so happy** tonight!' said the bloke.
He was right! When he went out of the bedroom, she **squirted it all over the doorknobs** and he couldn't get back in.

This bloke decides that his missus **isn't paying him enough attention** in the bedroom, so he strips down to just his shoes and parades around in front of her saying, '**Notice anything special about me?**' To which she replies, '**No, not really**.' 'Come on,' he says. 'Look again. It's pointing to my shoes!' To which she replies, 'Pity you didn't **keep your hat on** instead then, isn't it?!'

First new woman: 'My ultimate fantasy is to have two blokes at once!'
Second new woman: 'Me too! One for cooking, the other for cleaning!!

There were two old women in the park, just enjoying the day when a man comes up to them and **exposes himself**. One woman **has a stroke**… but the other **couldn't reach**!

The bride, upon her engagement, went to her mother and said, '**I've found a bloke just like father!**' Her mother replied, 'So what do you want from me – sympathy?'

First new woman (proudly):

'My bloke's an angel!'

Second new woman:

'You're lucky, mine's still alive.'

Young girl:

'Is it true, mum? I heard that in some parts of Africa a woman doesn't know her husband until she marries him?'

Mum:

'That happens in every country, dear!'

A **bloke lay dying.** His wife, Becky, was maintaining a candlelight vigil by his side. She held his fragile hand, tears running down her face. Her praying roused him from his slumber. He looked up and his pale lips began to move slightly.

'**My darling Becky**,' he whispered.

'**Hush, my love**,' she said. 'Rest. Shhh, don't talk.'

But he was insistent. 'Becky,' he said in his tired voice, 'I have something I must confess to you.'

'There's nothing to confess,' replied the weeping Becky.

'Everything's all right, go to sleep.'

'No, no. I must die in peace, Becky. I… **I slept with your sister**, your best friend, her best friend, and your mother!'

'**I know**,' Becky whispered softly…

'**That's why I poisoned you**'

A **fireman comes** home from work one day and tells his wife. 'You know, we have a wonderful system at the fire station: **BELL 1** rings and we all put on our jackets, **BELL 2** rings and we all slide down the pole, **BELL 3** rings and we're on the fire truck ready to go. From now on when I say **BELL 1**, I want you to strip naked. When I say **BELL 2**, I want you to jump in bed. And when I say **BELL 3**, we're going to make love all night.'

The next night he comes home from work and yells '**BELL 1**!' His wife promptly takes all her clothes off. Then he yells '**BELL 2**!' His wife jumps into bed. When he yells '**BELL 3**!' they begin making love. After a few minutes his wife yells '**BELL 4**!'

'What the hell is **BELL 4**?' asks the bloke.

'Roll out more hose,' she yells, 'You're nowhere near the fire!'

Two women are discussing their blokes over coffee one day.

'You know,' says the first. '**My bloke eats like a pig**, drinks like a fish and is a rat as well. In fact he makes me so sick I can barely eat.

'Why don't you chuck him?' says the other woman.

'Well,' says the first. 'I just want to lose another 6lbs...'

A **bloke** and his wife have a bitter quarrel on the day of their **40th wedding anniversary**. The bloke yells, 'When you die, I'm getting you a headstone that reads:

"Here Lies My Wife – Cold As Ever".'

'Oh yeah?' she replies. 'Well when you die, I'm getting you a headstone that reads:

"Here Lies My Husband – Stiff At Last"!'

A female computer consultant was helping a smug bloke set up his computer and asked him what word he'd like to use as a **password** to log in with. Wanting to embarrass the woman he told her to enter **PENIS**.
Without blinking or saying a word she entered the bloke's **password** – and then almost died laughing at the computer's response:

*** PASSWORD REJECTED. NOT LONG ENOUGH ***

A **bloke** was reading the paper when an ad caught his eye: '**£500 Porsche! New!**' The bloke figured it had to be a joke as no-one would sell a new Porsche for £500, but thought it was worth a shot. He goes to the advertiser's house and sure enough, the woman was selling an almost brand new Porsche.

'**Wow!**' the bloke says. 'Can I take it for a test drive?'

The car runs perfectly – he can see no catch – but he's still suspicious.

'Why are you selling me this great Porsche for only £500?'

And the woman replies: 'My husband just ran off with his secretary, and he told me I could have the house and the furniture as long as I sold his Porsche and sent him the money.'

A couple are having a few problems and agree to see a marriage counsellor. When the counsellor asks the woman why she thinks the relationship is over, the woman replies simply: '***Because he's a lousy lover***.'

The counsellor then asks the bloke what he thinks of this, and the bloke replies: '***How can she tell in three minutes?***'

9

GREAT MYSTERIES OF OUR TIME (III) – WHY?

Why are gingerbread men the best men of all?

They're cute. They're sweet. And if they give you any lip you can bite their heads off.

Why don't blokes eat more M&Ms?

They're too hard to peel!

Why have **blokes** made such a **mess** of this world?

They're waiting for women to pick up after them.

Why is marrying a bloke like going to a restaurant with a group of friends?

You order what you want, then when you see what the other person has, you wish you'd ordered that.

Why do blokes take showers and not baths?

Because weeing in the bath would be disgusting.

Why are blokes blokes and rats rats?

Because rats had first choice.

**Why can't a man
be both handsome
and intelligent?**

Because that would
make him a woman.

**Why is a bloke's brain
the size of a peanut?**

Because it is swollen.

**Why don't women get
married so often these days?**

Because they'd rather
have bacon in the fridge
than a pig in the living room.

Why is the bloke's intelligence worth more than the woman's?

It is rarer.

Why do blokes exist?

Who else is going to mow the lawn?

Why don't blokes go through menopause?

They never leave puberty.

Why do women close their eyes during sex?

They hate to see a
bloke enjoying himself!

Why won't women
ever be equal to blokes?

Because they'll never walk
down the street with a
bald head and a beer gut and
still think they're beautiful.

Why aren't all blokes annoying?

Because some of them are dead.

Why do blokes like love at first sight?

It saves them a lot of time.

Why do blokes like blonde jokes?

Because they can understand them.

Why don't blokes have mid-life crises?

They're stuck in adolescence.

Why is the book
Women Who Love Too Much
a disappointment for blokes?

There are no phone numbers in it.

Why do blokes have
see-through lunch boxes?

So they can tell whether they're going to work or coming home again.

Why are computers
better than blokes?

They don't fart, they don't talk endlessly about footy, and they're always going down on you!

Why are blokes proof of reincarnation?

You can't get that dumb in one lifetime!

Why do blokes with a pierced ear make the best boyfriends?

Because they're used to pain and know how to buy jewellery.

Why is it a waste of time telling a bloke to go to hell?

Because he'd get lost on the way.

10

IF MEN ARE FROM MARS AND WOMEN ARE FROM VENUS – BLOKES ARE FROM URANUS…

A bloke is walking down the beach and comes across an old bottle. He picks it up, pulls out the cork and **out pops a genie**.

The genie says, 'Thank you for freeing me from the bottle. In return **I will grant you three wishes**.'

The bloke says 'Great! I always dreamed of this and I know exactly what I want. First, **I want one billion dollars in a Swiss bank account**.' Poof!

There is a flash of light and a piece of paper with account numbers appears in the bloke's hand. He continues, 'Next, **I want a brand new red Ferrari** right here.' Poof! There is a flash of light and a bright red brand-new Ferrari appears right next to him. He continues, '**Finally, I want to be irresistible to women**.' Poof! There is a flash of light and he turns into a **box of chocolates**.

If one bloke can wash one stack of dishes in one hour, how many stacks of dishes could four blokes wash in four hours?

None. They'd all sit down together to watch the footy.

A bloke is staying in a hotel. 'And will there be anything else, sir?,' the bellboy asks after setting out an elaborate dinner for two. 'No thank you,' says the bloke, 'that will be all.' As the bellboy turns to leave he notices a beautiful satin **negligee** on the bed.

'Anything for **your wife**?' he asks.

'Oh yeah! That's a good idea,' the bloke says.

'Bring me a postcard.'

A bloke has been visiting Cuba for a week. He's leaving the next day and still hasn't **tried the local food**, so he goes to a restaurant and sits down to order, then sees the bloke next to him eating a delicious meal. Calling the waiter over he asks for the same meal, but the waiter says there's none left. The bloke asks him what it is and the waiter replies: '**That is the testicles from the bull that lost** the fight earlier that morning, if you come back tomorrow we'll save the dish for you.' So the bloke goes back the next day and the waiter has his food prepared for him. He eats the meal and calls the waiter over: '**This meal was delicious**, the only thing is it seemed a lot smaller than the one the bloke yesterday was eating.' And the waiter replies: '**Ah, sorry sir, sometimes the bull wins.**'

Two blokes were trying to get in a quick **18 holes of golf** but there were **two terrible women golfers** in front of them who were hitting the ball **all over the place** and **holding up the two blokes**. The first bloke says to his mate, 'Why don't you go over and ask if we can play through?' His mate agrees and gets about halfway over to the women, turns around sharpish and walks back to his mate. The first bloke says, '**What's wrong?**' His mate says, '**One of them is my wife and the other is my mistress**.' The first bloke says, 'Oh, that's a problem. I'll go over.' He too gets about halfway there, turns around and walks back. His mates says, 'What's wrong now?' The first bloke says, '**Small world.**'

A **drunk** is standing **peeing into a fountain** in the middle of town, so a **policeman** goes up to him and says: 'Stop that right now and put it away.' The drunk **puts his willy back into his trousers** and does up the zip. As the policeman turns to walk away the drunk starts to laugh. 'OK,' says the cop. '**What's so funny?**' 'Fooled you,' says the drunk. '**I may have put it away, but I didn't stop!**'

A **bloke** is sitting in the **first class section** on a plane to Africa but his ticket is only for **economy class** so the air hostess asks him to move. The bloke refuses, saying: 'I have a good job and pay all my taxes. **I deserve to sit in first class**.' After about 10 minutes of arguing the head air hostess comes and asks him to move. He refuses saying: 'I have a good job and pay all my taxes. I deserve to sit in first class.' After about another 10 minutes of arguing the pilot comes and whispers in the bloke's ear and he moves and sits at the rear of the plane. When the hostesses ask the pilot what he said, he answers: '**I told him the front half of the plane doesn't go to Africa**.'

In a transatlantic flight, a plane passes through a **severe storm**. The **turbulence is awful**, and things go from bad to worse when one wing is **struck by lightning**.

One woman in particular loses it. Screaming, she stands up in the front of the plane. '**I'm too young to die!**' she wails. 'But if I have to die, I want my last minutes to be memorable! I've had plenty of lovers in my life, but no-one has ever made me really feel like a woman! **Is there ANYONE on this plane who can make me feel like a WOMAN?**'

For a moment there's silence. Everyone has forgotten their own peril, and they all stare, riveted, at the desperate woman. Then a man stands up in the rear of the plane. '**I can make you feel like a woman**,' he says.

He's gorgeous. Tall, well-built, with long, flowing black hair and jet black eyes. He starts to walk slowly up the aisle, unbuttoning his shirt one button at a time. No-one moves. The woman is breathing heavily in anticipation as the stranger approaches. **He removes his shirt**. Muscles ripple across his chest as he reaches her, and extends the arm holding his shirt to the trembling woman, and whispers...

'**Iron this**.'

Grandpa was celebrating his **100th** birthday and everybody complimented him on how athletic and well-preserved he appeared.

'**Gentlemen, I will tell you the secret of my success**,' he cackled. 'I have walked for at least an hour in the open air day after day for some 75 years now.'

The celebrants were impressed and asked how he managed to keep up his rigorous fitness regime.

'Well, you see, my wife and I were married 75 years ago. **On our wedding night**, we made a solemn pledge. Whenever **we had a fight**, the one who was proved wrong would go outside and take a walk...'

A **couple** take their young son to the circus, and while the bloke's buying popcorn the boy asks: '**Mum, what's that long thing on the elephant?**'

'That's the elephant's trunk, dear,' she replies

'No, mum. **Down underneath**.'

The woman blushes and says: 'Oh, that. That's nothing.'

The boy's dad returns, and his mum goes off to get a coke.

As soon as she leaves, the boy repeats his question.

'That's the elephant's trunk, son,' the bloke answers.

'Dad, I know what a trunk is. **What's the thing down there?**'

The bloke looks and says: 'Oh, that's the **elephant's penis**.'

'Dad,' the boy says. 'How come when I asked mum, she said it was nothing?'

The bloke takes a deep breath and explains: **Son, I've spoiled that woman**.'

When does a bloke open the car door for his wife?

a) when he's got a new car.
b) when he's got a new wife.

Once upon a time a female **brain cell** accidentally ended up in a **bloke's head**. She looked around nervously but it was all empty and quiet. '**Hello**?' she cried, but no-one answered.

'Is there anyone here?' she cried a little louder, but still no answer came. The female brain cell started to feel alone and scared and yelled: '**HELLO, IS THERE ANYONE HERE**?'

Then she heard a voice from far, far away: '**Hello, we're down here...**'

A **bloke is stranded** on a desert island with Pamela Anderson. Out of sheer loneliness the relationship becomes physical and for four months they enjoy **glorious sex**. Then one day the bloke says to her: 'Can I borrow your eyebrow pencil to **draw a moustache on you?**' 'I suppose so,' says Pamela. 'Would you wear some of my clothes and let me call you Bill?' he asks. Reluctantly she agrees. Then he grabs her by the arm and says: '**Hey Bill, you won't believe who I've been sleeping with** these last four months!'

A **bloke** gets home early from work and hears strange **noises coming from the bedroom**. He rushes upstairs to find his **wife naked on the bed**, sweating and panting. '**What's up?**' he says. '**I'm having a heart attack**,' cries the woman. He rushes downstairs to grab the phone, but just as he's dialling, his four-year-old son comes up and says 'Daddy! Daddy! Uncle Ted's hiding in your wardrobe and **he's got no clothes on!**' The bloke slams the phone down and storms upstairs into the bedroom, past his screaming wife, and rips open the wardrobe door. Sure enough, there's his brother, totally naked, cowering on the wardrobe floor. '**You rotten bastard**,' says the bloke. '**My wife's having a heart attack** and you're running around naked scaring the kids!'

A **married bloke** is having an affair with his **secretary**. One day, their passions overcome them and they take off for her house, where they make **passionate love all afternoon**. Exhausted from the **wild sex**, they fall asleep, awakening around 8.00pm. As the man throws on his clothes, he tells the woman to **take his shoes** outside and **rub through through with grass and dirt**.

Mystified, she nevertheless complies. He slips into his shoes and drives home. 'Where have you been!' demands his wife when he enters the house.

'Darling, I can't lie to you. **I've been having an affair** with my secretary, and we've been having sex all afternoon. I fell asleep and didn't wake up until 8.00pm.'

The wife glances down at his shoes and says, 'You lying bastard! **You've been playing golf!**'

A **bloke** was shipwrecked on a desert island for a whole year. Then one day a **stunning blonde** walks out of the sea dressed in scuba gear and lays down on the sand next to him. '**Would you like a cigarette?**' she asks. '**Of course**,' says the bloke – amazed as she unzips a pocket of the wetsuit, produces a pack of Marlboro, lights it seductively and passes it to him. '**How about a beer?**' she asks next. 'This is incredible,' says the bloke as she unzips another pocket of the wetsuit and produces a **chilled can of Stella** and two glasses, pouring them both a drink.

The blonde gets even closer to the bloke now and presses herself against him saying: '**And do you fancy playing around?**'

'Oh God,' says the bloke, thinking he's gone to heaven. '**Don't say you've got a set of golf clubs** in there too!'

A **bloke** spots a lamp by the roadside. He picks it up, rubs it vigorously, and suddenly **a genie appears**.

'I'll grant you **your fondest wish**,' says the genie.

The bloke thinks for a moment then says: 'I want a spectacular job – a job that no man has ever succeeded at or has ever attempted to do.'

'**Poof!**' says the genie. '**You're a housewife**.'

A **small boy** is lost at a large shopping mall. He approaches a uniformed policeman and says, '**I've lost my dad!**'

The policeman asks, '**What's he like?**' And the little boy replies, '**Beer and women with big boobs.**'

11

WHAT ARE THEY LIKE?! (I)

Why are blokes like microwaves?

They both get hot in 15 seconds.

Why are blokes like dolphins?

They are both said to be intelligent, but no-one can prove it.

Why are blokes like video recorders?

They go forwards, backwards, forwards, backwards, stop and eject.

Why are blokes like a parking space?

Because all the best ones are taken and the rest are too small!

Why are blokes like chocolate?

The richer the better.

Why are blokes like a deck of cards?

You need a heart to love them, a diamond to marry them, a club to beat them and a spade to bury the bugger!

Why is a bloke like a clothes drier?

A 15 minute tumble and they're done.

Why are blokes like clouds?

**Eventually they
bugger off and
it's a really nice day!**

**Why are the best blokes
like toilet paper?**

Soft, strong and –
most of all –
disposable.

Why are blokes like decaffeinated coffee?

Neither of them will keep you going all night.

12

WHAT'S THE DIFFERENCE, ANYWAY? (I)

What's the **difference** between a **bloke** and a **pig**?

A pig doesn't turn into a bloke after two pints of lager!

What's the difference between hard and dark?

It stays dark all night.

What's the **difference** between a **bloke** and a **shopping trolley**?

Sometimes a shopping trolley has a mind of its own.

What's the difference between a bloke and childbirth?

One can be terribly painful and sometimes almost unbearable while the other is only having a baby.

What's the difference between a bloke and a bloke's photo?

The photo is fully developed.

What's the difference between a bar and a clitoris?

Most blokes have no trouble finding a bar.

What's the difference between a bloke and a computer?

You only have to punch the information into a computer once.

What's the difference between a woman and a computer?

A computer doesn't laugh at a 3.5-inch floppy.

What's the difference between an attractive man and an ugly man?

About 10 glasses of wine.

What is the difference between your husband and your lover?

About four hours.

What's the difference between light and hard?

A bloke can sleep with a light on.

What's the difference between a bloke
and a piece of cheese?

Cheese matures.

What's the **difference** between a **golf ball** and a **G-spot**?

Men will always look for a golf ball.

What's the difference between single women
and married women?

Single women go home, see what's in the fridge then
go to bed. Married women go home, see what's in
the bed then go to the fridge!

What's the **difference** between a **porcupine** and a **sports car**?

A porcupine has pricks on the outside.

What's the difference between *Match Of The Day* and the toilet seat?

A bloke never will never miss *Match Of The Day*.

What's the difference between a bloke and a battery?

A battery has a positive side!

What's the difference between a single 40-year-old woman and a single 40-year-old bloke?

The 40-year-old woman often thinks of having children and the 40-year-old bloke often thinks about dating them.

What's the **difference** between a **new husband** and a **new dog**?

After a year, the dog is still excited to see you.

13

EVERYONE LIKES A LIST, DON'T THEY? (II)

Seminars For Men

- Combating Stupidity.
- Understanding Your Financial Incompetence.

Reasons To
Give Flowers

- How To Stay Awake After Sex.
- Why The Weekend And Sports Are Not Synonymous.
- The Morning Dilemma – If It's Awake, Take A Shower?
- Helpful Postural Hints For Couch Potatoes.
- How Not To Act Younger Than Your Children.
- The Remote Control – Overcoming Your Dependency.

- How To Take Illness Like An Adult.
- You – The Weaker Sex.
- PMS – Learning When To Keep Your Mouth Shut.
- You Too Can Do Housework.
- How To Fill An Ice Cube Tray.
- We Do Not Want Sleazy Underthings For Christmas
  – Give Us Money.

Wonderful Laundry
Techniques (formerly called
'Don't Wash My Silks').

- Understanding The Female Response To Your Coming In Drunk At 4 a.m.
- Parenting – No, It Doesn't End With Conception.
- Get A Life – Learn How To Cook.
- How Not To Act Like An Idiot When You Are Obviously Wrong.

Why blokes are like computers

- They have a lot of data but are still clueless.
- A better model is always just around the corner.
- They look nice and shiny until you bring them home.
- It's always necessary to have a back-up.
- They'll do whatever you say if you push the right buttons.
- The best part of having one is the games you can play.
- They get hot when you turn them on – and that's the only time you get their full attention.
- The lights are on but nobody's home.
- Big power surges knock them out for the night.
- Size does matter.
- They're heavily dependant on external tools and equipment.
- They periodically cut you off when you think you've established a network connection.

If blokes had PMS, what would happen?

The Government would allocate funds to study it.

•

Cramps would become an acceptable reason to apply for permanent disability.

•

There would be a bank holiday every 28 days.

•

All of the above.

Why blokes like e-mail
(clue: it's because it's like a penis)

- In the not-too-distant past, it was just a way to transmit information considered vital to the survival of the species. Now it's just used for fun.
- Once they've started playing with it, it's hard to stop.
- It can be up or down. It's more fun when it's up but it makes it hard to get any real work done.
- It provides a way to interact with people.
- Those who have it would be devastated if it were cut off.
- It has no conscience and no memory. Left to its own devices, it'll do the same dumb things it did before.
- If they're not careful what they do with it, it can land them in big trouble.

Cutting put-downs for blokes who really deserve them

- 'You're like my blender – I wanted it at the time, but I can't remember why.'
- 'I'll see you in my dreams … if I eat too much cheese.'
- 'There was something I liked about you … but the thing is, you've spent it now.'
- 'Darling, no one could love you as much as you do.'
- 'Sleeping with you has made me realise how much I miss my ex.'
- 'It's a shame your parents didn't practise safe sex.'
- 'You're proof enough that I can take a joke.'
- 'The only thing you could be committed to is a mental institution.'

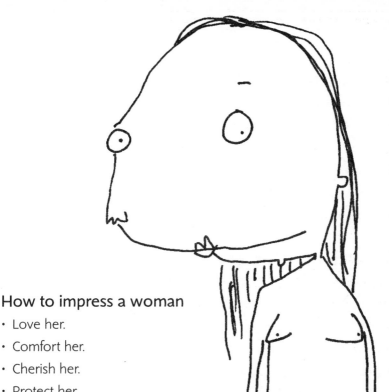

How to impress a woman

- Love her.
- Comfort her.
- Cherish her.
- Protect her.
- Kiss her.
- Cuddle her.
- Listen to her.
- Support her.
- Compliment her.
- Respect her.
- Care for her.

How to impress a bloke:

- Show up naked.
- Bring beer.

Show up naked, bring beer

What to say to annoying blokes who ask: 'Why aren't you married yet?'

- 'What? And spoil my great sex life?'
- 'Just lucky, I guess.'
- 'I wouldn't want my parents to drop dead from sheer happiness.'
- 'We really want to, but my lover's wife just won't go for it.'
- 'I'm waiting till I get to your age.'
- 'My fiancé is waiting for his parole.'
- 'What? And share my trust fund millions?'

Why Santa can't possibly be a bloke.

- Blokes can't pack a bag.
- Most blokes would die rather than be seen wearing red velvet.
- Blokes don't answer letters.
- Blokes aren't interested in stockings unless someone's wearing them.
- The 'ho, ho, ho' thing would seriously inhibit a bloke's pulling power.
- Being totally responsible for Christmas would require commitment.

The medical-sounding notice that might just stop your bloke rolling in drunk at 3 a.m. talking shite.

WARNING: Consumption of alcohol ...

- ... may make you think you're whispering when you're not.
- ... may cause you to thay shings like thish.
- ... may lead you to believe that ex-lovers are dying for you to phone them at 4 a.m.
- ... may leave you wondering what the hell happened to your trousers.
- ... may make you think you do indeed have mystical Kung Fu powers.
- ... is the leading cause of inexplicable carpet burns on your forehead.
- ... may create the illusion that you're tougher, handsomer and smarter than some really, really big bloke called Baz.
- ... may cause a glitch in the space/time continuum, whereby small (and large) gaps of time disappear.
- ... may actually cause pregnancy.
- ... may make you think you can logically converse with members of the opposite sex without spitting.
- ... may cause you to roll over in the morning and see something really scary (whose species and/or name you can't remember.
- ... may lead you to think people are laughing with you, not at you.

Harsh things a woman can say to a naked bloke ...

Wow ... and your feet are so big!

•

I guess this makes me the early bird!

•

But it still works – right?

•

Are you cold?

•

Maybe if we water it, it'll grow.

•

Why don't we just cuddle?

•

You know they have surgery to fix that.

•

Why is God punishing me?

•

I never saw one like that before.

•

Maybe it looks better in natural light?

Wow … and your feet are so big!

GREAT MYSTERIES OF OUR TIME (IV) – WHY?

Why is a **computer** like a **penis**?

If you don't apply the appropriate protective measures, it can spread viruses.

Why is it difficult to find blokes who are sensitive, caring and good looking?

They all have boyfriends already.

Why do blokes like masturbation?

Because it's sex with someone they love.

Why did the man cross the road?

He heard the chicken was a slut.

Why don't women blink during foreplay?

They don't have time.

Why do black widow spiders kill their males after mating?

To stop the snoring before it starts.

Why is sleeping with a bloke like a soap opera?

Just when it's getting interesting,
they're finished until next time.

Why do blokes have a penis and a brain?

No one knows – there isn't enough blood to supply
both at the same time.

Why should you never let your bloke's mind wander?

Because it's too little to be let out alone.

Why do **blokes** find it **difficult** to make **eye contact**?

Breasts don't have eyes.

Why will a woman rarely make a fool of a man?

Most of them are the do-it-yourself types.

Why go for younger men?
You might as well – they never mature anyway.

Why should you never worry about doing housework?
No bloke ever made love to a woman because the house was spotless?

Why do blokes name their penises?
Because they wouldn't trust a stranger with 90 per cent of their decisions.

Why are all dumb blonde jokes one-liners?
So blokes can remember them.

Why is a bloke's penis like the Rubik's cube?
The more you play with it the harder it gets.

Why is it that a single woman doesn't fart?

She doesn't get an asshole till she gets married.

Why are **women** so **bad** at **mathematics**?

Because blokes keep telling them that this I--------I is 12 inches.

Why is it good that there are women astronauts?
So that when the crew gets lost in space, at least the women will ask for directions.

Why don't blokes often show their true feelings?
Because they don't have feelings.

Why would women be better off if blokes treated them like cars?
At least then they would get a little attention every 6 months or 5,000 miles, whichever came first.

Why do doctors slap babies' bums right after they're born?
To knock the penises off the clever ones.

Why is food better than men?
Because you don't have to wait an hour for seconds.

Why do blokes like BMWs?
They can spell it.

Why do blokes have a hole in their penis?

So they can get air to their brain.

Why do blokes have their best ideas during sex?

Because they're plugged into a genius!

Why did the man cross the road?

Because he got his knob stuck in the chicken!

Why do blokes always look stupid?

Because they are stupid.

Why did the man cross the road?

Never mind that! What's he doing out of the kitchen!!

Why is psychoanalysis quicker for blokes than for women?

When it's time to go back to childhood,
they're already there.

Why do only 10 per cent of blokes go to heaven?

Because if there were any more it would be hell.

Why do blokes hate wearing condoms?

It cuts off the circulation to their brain.

Why can't **blokes** make **pancakes**?

Because they're useless tossers!

Why do women rub their eyes when they wake up?

Because they don't have balls to scratch.

Why is wee yellow and sperm white?

So a bloke can tell if he's coming or going.

Why did the condom go flying across the room?

It was pissed off.

Why shouldn't you chain a bloke to the sink?

He won't be able to reach the ironing.

Why do women fake orgasms?

Because blokes fake foreplay!

Why do blokes go bald?

To stop them having any more crap hair cuts!!!

Why do blokes buy electric lawnmowers?

So they can find their way back to the house.

Why don't blokes use toilet paper?

Because God made them perfect arses!

IF YOU CALL A SPADE A SPADE, WHAT DO YOU CALL A BLOKE?

What do you **call** a **handcuffed bloke**?

Trustworthy.

What do you call a bloke with 90 per cent of his intelligence gone?

Divorced.

What do you call a bloke who expects sex on the second date?

Slow.

What do you call a woman who does the same amount of work as a bloke?

A lazy cow.

What do you call a bloke with half a brain?

Gifted.

What do you call 200 blokes at the bottom of the sea?

A good start.

What do you call a woman who knows where her husband is every night?

A widow.

What do you call a bloke with 99 per cent of his brain missing?

Castrated.

What do you call 144 blokes in a room?

Gross stupidity.

What do you call **twelve naked blokes**, sitting on each other's **shoulders**?

A scrotum pole.

What do you call a woman without an arse?

Single.

What do you call the useless flap of skin on the end of a penis?

A bloke!

What do you call a musician without a girlfriend?

Homeless.

16

IT'S A BIBLE THING! (II)

How do we know **God** is a **man**?

Because if God were a woman, sperm would taste
like chocolate.

On the day the good Lord was handing out sex lives, he gave man 20 years of a normal sex life and man protested very loudly. The Lord then gave the monkey 20 years, but the monkey said: 'Lord, 20 years is too much, I only need 10.' Man was standing nearby and overheard. He said to the monkey: 'Can I have the other 10?' and the monkey agreed. Then it was the lion's turn and the Lord also gave the lion 20 years, but the lion assured the Lord he too only needed 10. Man again jumped in and asked for the other 10 and the lion agreed. It was then the donkey's turn and the Lord also gave him 20 years, but he too stated he only needed 10 and of course man requested the donkey's remaining 10 which he got. That explains why blokes spend 20 years having a normal sex life, the next 10 years monkeying around, then the next 10 years lying about, and the last 10 years making asses of themselves.

Why did God make man before woman?

You need a rough draft before you make a final copy.

On the eighth day God was looking down over his creation
when he spotted Adam and Eve in the Garden of Eden.

He says to them: 'I've got a couple of leftovers which
I might as well hand out to you. I can't decide who should
have what, so the person who shouts loudest gets the
first choice. The first item is a thing that allows you to
pee standing up.'

Adam immediately jumps up and down shouting:
'Me, me, I want that.' So God gives it to him.

'Damn,' thinks Eve. 'That sounds really good.
I should have shouted louder.'
'Oh well,' says God. 'I'm afraid all I have left is
this multiple orgasm.'

Bill Clinton and the Pope died on the same day but there was a
mix-up and Bill Clinton went to Heaven and the Pope went to Hell.
The Devil was well pissed off because he wanted to tell Bill Clinton
jokes about shagging secretaries. So he phones up God and tells
him that they'd better swap the Pope and Bill around. The next day
they pass each other and the Pope says to Bill: 'I'm so glad I'm
finally going to Heaven. I can't wait to meet the Virgin Mary.'
And Bill Clinton says: 'Oops!!!'

Why was **Moses** wandering **through** the desert for **40 years**?

**Because blokes refuse
to ask for directions!**

Three blokes arrive at the gates of Heaven, and are greeted by St Peter. He says to the first man: 'Have you been a good person?' The first man replies: 'Yes, I've led a truly worthwhile life, and I've never been unfaithful to my wife.' So St Peter gives him a Rolls Royce car to aid his travels in Heaven.

Then St Peter asks the second man if he's led a good life. The second man replies: 'Well, mostly I've been honest and caring, but I have been unfaithful to my wife once.'

'Very well,' replies St Peter. 'You may have a Ford Fiesta.'

He goes to the third man and asks him the same question, to which the man replies: 'Well, no. I've stolen from my loved ones, and I've not been faithful to my wife for more than a week.' So St Peter gives the third man a bicycle.

A few days later, the second man and the third

man pass the first man, who's in his gleaming

Rolls Royce, sobbing his heart out. The second

man asks him: 'What's the matter? If I had your

car I'd be the happiest man here!'

'I was,' he replies, 'but I've just seen my wife,

and she was on roller-skates.'

What did God say after creating man?

I must be able to do better than that.

C ontrary to the teachings of the Bible, God created Eve first. She was intelligent, beautiful and interesting ... and had three breasts! After a few days God came to check on her and she complained that the third breast was a bit uncomfortable, so he said: 'OK we'll throw one away.' This made Eve happy.

Over the next few months she wandered around seeing other animals strolling around in twos and said: 'God, I feel lonely. I need a man.' And God said: 'No problem. Tell me now, where did I throw that useless tit?'

The Lad's Prayer.

Our beer

Which art in barrels

Hallowed be thy drink

Thy will be drunk

I will be drunk

At home as it is in the local

Forgive us this day our daily spillage

As we forgive those that spillest against us

And lead us not into the poncey practise of wine tasting

And deliver us from alco-pops

For mine is the bitter

The ale and the lager

For ever and ever

Barmen.

Why did **God** put **blokes** on **Earth**?

Because a vibrator can't mow the lawn.

17

GREAT MYSTERIES OF OUR TIME (V) – WHAT'S ALL THAT ABOUT?

What do you **instantly know** about a **well-dressed bloke**?

His wife is good at picking out clothes.

What part of a bloke grows, the more you stroke it?

His ego.

What do electric trains and breasts have in common?

They're intended for children, but it's blokes who usually end up playing with them.

What do blokes consider house cleaning?

Lifting their feet so you can vacuum under them.

What have you got if you have 100 blokes buried up to their necks in sand?

Not enough sand.

What's a bloke's idea of a romantic evening out?

A candlelit football stadium.

What are a woman's four favourite animals?

A mink in the wardrobe, a Jaguar in the garage, a tiger in the bedroom and an ass who'll pay for it all.

What do you have when you've got two little balls in your hand?

A bloke's undivided attention.

What's the best way to get a bloke to do something?

Suggest he's too old for it.

What is the one thing that all blokes at singles bars have in common?

They're married.

What should you do if your **bloke walks out**?

Shut the door after him.

What is a **bloke's** view of **safe sex**?

A padded headboard.

What's the only time a bloke thinks about a candlelit dinner?

When the power goes off.

What's the definition of a bachelor?

A bloke who's missed the opportunity
to make a woman miserable.

What's a bloke's idea of foreplay?

Half an hour of begging.

What's the best time to try and change a bloke?

When he's in nappies.

What should you **reply** if a **bloke** asks you: '**Am I your first?**'

'You could be, you look familiar.'

What are the two reasons blokes don't mind their own business?

i) No mind. ii) No business.

What's the best thing to come out of a penis when you stroke it?

The wrinkles.

What are the measurements of the perfect husband?

82-20-45. That's 82 years old, £20 million in the bank and a 45-degree fever.

What's a world without blokes?

A world full of fat, happy women.

What does a **bloke** consider a **seven course meal**?

A hot dog and a six-pack of beer.

What do **fat blokes** and **mopeds** have in **common**?

They're both a good ride, but you'd die if your mates saw you on one!

What does the smart bloke do in an M&M factory?

Proofread.

What's the **thinnest** book
in the **world**?

What Blokes Know About Women.

What's a bloke's definition of a
romantic evening?

Sex.

What do a **clitoris**, an **anniversary**,
and a **toilet** have in **common**?

Blokes always miss them.

What does a bloke have to do
to keep you interested in his company?

Own it!

What does a **girl** have to say to
seduce a **bloke**?

'Hi.'

18

SO THIS BLOKE GOES INTO A PUB...(II)

A bloke goes into a supermarket and buys a tube of toothpaste, a bottle of Pepsi, a bag of tortilla chips, and a frozen pizza. The cute girl at the register looks at him and says: 'Single, huh?' Sarcastically the bloke sneers: 'How'd you guess?' She replies: 'Because you're ugly.'

A bloke staggers home at 3 a.m. after a pub-crawl. On finding his wife awake and naked in bed he decides to show some interest. He gently kisses her on the forehead but no response. He then softly kisses her lips still no response. Moving downwards he caresses her neck and then brushes his lips expertly across each breast, before continuing slowly downward with his tongue until it finds a haven exploring her navel. No reaction whatsoever. His next move is to bend right down and kiss inside her right thigh just above her knee. At that moment his wife sits bolt upright and screams: 'If it had been a pub you wouldn't have missed it!'

A bloke was trying to decide which of three women he would ask to marry him. He gave them each £1000.

The first spent £900 on clothes, and put £100 in the bank.

The second spent £500 on clothes and put £500 in the bank.

The third spent £100 on clothes and put £900 in the bank.

Which one did he choose?

The one with the big breasts.

A bloke goes to the doctors and says: 'Doctor, doctor, you've got to help me. I've got six willies!'

The doctor looks at him in disbelief:

'That's a load of bollocks!!'

T wo women are talking on the phone.

One says to the other:

'Hang on a minute, the old man popped down the garden ages ago to get a cabbage for dinner and he's not come back. I'd better look for him.'

When she comes back to the phone she says:

'Oh no! He's dropped dead in the vegetable patch.'

'What are you going to do now?' her friend replies. Quick as a flash she says: 'Damn. I'll have to open a tin of peas!'

A woman goes into a card shop and stands for a long time staring at the specialist cards, finally shaking her head,

'No.' Eventually a shop assistant comes over and asks if he can help.

'I don't know,' said the woman. 'Do you have any "Sorry I laughed at your dick" cards?'

Three blokes are discussing the control they have over their wives.

The first bloke says: 'I have immense control over my wife. Every night I come home from work to find my dinner waiting for me on the table.'

The second bloke says: 'I have total control over my wife. Every night I come home from work to find a hot bath ready and waiting.'

The third bloke says: 'The other night, lads, my wife came to me on her hands and knees.'

The other two are really impressed with this and ask: 'Yeah? what did she say?'

'GET OUT FROM UNDER THAT BED AND FIGHT LIKE A MAN!!!'

A woman goes into a shop to buy a wedding dress – for her fourth wedding. She chooses a traditional white dress, which surprises the sales assistant.

'Oh but I'm still a virgin,' the woman replies.

'How can that be,' says the sales assistant, 'if this is to be your fourth wedding.'

'My first husband was a psychologist he just wanted to talk about it; my second husband was a gynaecologist he just wanted to look at it; my third husband was a stamp collector... God I loved him!'

A nun walks onto a bus, which is empty except for the driver. The nun says to the driver: 'I'm going to die soon but I want three wishes fulfilled before I do. Firstly, I want to have sex, but I must die a virgin, so the sex has to be anal. Secondly, I cannot commit adultery, so the bloke I sleep with has to be single. Finally, the bloke has to be a stranger to me and must not tell anyone else.'

The nun then asks the bus driver if he thinks he's up to fulfilling the wishes.

The bus driver readily agrees and takes the nun upstairs, promptly fulfilling the first wish, but afterwards he feels very guilty and says to the nun: 'I'm afraid I've lied to you, I am in fact married with three children.'

The nun replies: 'That's OK, I've lied too. My name's Kevin and I'm off to a fancy dress party!'

A bloke goes to see his doctor for a check-up. During the examination the doctor notices the bloke's yellow penis. The doctor asks him a few questions. 'Do you work with chemicals, young man?'

'No,' replies the bloke, 'I'm unemployed.'

'Well do you smoke?' asks the doctor.

'No, I don't smoke,' says the bloke.

By now the doctor is a bit perplexed. 'But how did you get a yellow penis, then?'

'I dunno,' replies the man. 'I just sit at home all day, watching porno videos and eating cheesy puffs.'

A bloke picks up a female partner at the golf club. She cleans him out, and as compensation takes him home and gives him the mother and father of all blowjobs. He's so pleased that he asks for a return match and the same thing happens several times.

Next time, he suggests they have full sex, but she admits that she's actually a bloke in the process of a sex change. When he goes wild, the transsexual asks why he's so angry when he clearly enjoyed the blowjobs.

The bloke replies: 'Never mind the blowjobs. You've been playing off the ladies' tees!'

A bloke and a woman are strolling down a beach on a romantic moonlit night. Gently the bloke takes the woman's hand and asks her to close her eyes. He then places her hand on his crotch. To which she retorts: 'No thanks, I don't smoke.'

Two sperm are swimming along happily. One sperm says to the other: 'How much further have we got to swim before we get to that egg?'

'I dunno, mate,' says the other sperm. 'We've only just passed the tonsils.'

A bloke is driving up a steep, narrow mountain road. A woman is driving down the same road. As they pass each other, the woman leans out of the window and yells: 'PIG!!' The bloke immediately leans out of his window and replies: 'BITCH!!' They each continue on their way, and as the bloke rounds the next corner, he crashes into a pig in the middle of the road. If only blokes would listen.

A bloke walks into a pub and asks the barman for six double whiskies. The Barman looks shocked: 'Six double whiskies, that's an awful lot for someone who's come in on his own!'

'But I've just had my first blowjob,' replies the man.

'In that case have another one on the house,' states the barman. 'Well,' says the bloke, 'If six doesn't take the taste away, I don't think seven will!'

A couple are having a blazing row, and things are starting to get personal. 'I don't know why you wear a bra,' says the bloke. 'You haven't got anything to put in there!' The woman stares at him in disbelief: 'Well you wear pants, don't you?'

A bloke walks into a bar, and says to the barman: 'I'd like an orange juice please.'

The barman says: 'Still?'

The bloke says: 'Well I haven't changed my fucking mind!'

A n intelligent woman, an intelligent bloke and the tooth fairy were walking down the road one day when they looked down and noticed a £5 note on the pavement. Which one picked the £5 note up?

The intelligent woman of course ... the other two don't exist!

19

WHAT ARE THEY LIKE?! (II)

Why are blokes like floor tiles?

Lay them right the first time, and you can walk all over them for the rest of your life!

Why are **boring blokes** like **snot**?

They get up your nose.

Why are **blokes** like **cool bags**?

Load them with beer and you can take them anywhere.

Why are blokes like high heels?

They're easy to walk on once you get the hang of it.

Why are **blokes** like **horoscopes**?

They always tell you what to do and are usually wrong.

Why are blokes like bank accounts?

Without a lot of money, they don't generate much interest.

Why are **blokes** like lawn **mowers**?

If you're not pushing one around, then you're riding it.

Why are blokes like used cars?

Both are easy-to-get, cheap, and unreliable.

Why are **blokes** like **chocolate bars**?

They're sweet, smooth, and they usually head right for your hips.

Why are **blokes** like **holidays**?

They never seem to be long enough.

Why are blokes like mascara?

They usually run at the first sign of emotion.

Why are **blokes** like **place-mats**?

They only show up when there's food on the table.

Why are blokes like lava lamps?

Fun to look at, but not all that bright.

Why are blokes like cement?

After getting laid, they take a long time to get hard.

Why are blokes like plungers?

They spend most of their lives in a hardware store or the bathroom.

Why are **blokes** like **blenders**?

You need one, but you don't know why.

Why are blokes like toilets?

Because they're always either engaged, vacant or full of crap.

Why are **blokes** like **beer bottles**?

Because they're both empty from the neck up!

Why are blokes like popcorn?

They satisfy you, but only for a little while.

Why are **blokes** like **bike helmets**?

Handy in an emergency, but otherwise they just LOOK SILLY.

Why are **blokes** like **parking spaces**?

Because the good ones are always gone and the only ones left are disabled.

Why are blokes like coffee?

The best ones are rich, warm, and can keep you up all night long.

Why are **blokes** like **spray paint**?

One squeeze and they're all over you.

Why are blokes like cashpoint machines?

Once they withdraw they lose interest.

Why are blokes like caravans?

Because they follow wherever you take them.

Why are **blokes** like **laxatives**?

They both irritate the shit out of you.

Why are blokes like sperms?

They both have only a one in a million chance of becoming a human being.

Why are **blokes** like **computers**?

You never know how much they mean to you until they go down on you.

Why are blokes like a snowstorm?

'Cos you don't know when they're coming, how long they're going to last or how many inches you'll get!

Why are **blokes** like **department stores**?

Their clothes should always be half off.

Why are blokes like dog poos?

The older they get the easier they are to pick up!

20

GREAT MYSTERIES OF OUR TIME (VI) – HOW COME?

How do you drown a muscle man?

You put a mirror in a pool!

How can you tell the difference between blokes' real gifts and their guilt gifts?

Guilt gifts are nicer.

How many **blokes** does it **take** to change a **toilet roll**?

Who knows, it hasn't happened yet!

How are blokes like noodles?

They're always in hot water, they lack taste,
and they need dough.

How can you **keep** a **bloke happy**?

Who cares?

How many blokes does it take to tile a bathroom?

One – if you slice him thinly enough.

How many **blokes** does it take to **screw** in a **lightbulb**?

One ... men will screw anything.

How come blokes have such small balls?

Because so very few of them can dance.

How do you stop a bloke from drowning?

Take your foot off his head.

How do you get a **bloke** to do **sit-ups**?

Put the remote control between his toes.

How can you tell if a bloke is well-hung?

You can't get your finger between the rope and his neck.

How do you know when a **bloke** is **gonna** say **something clever**?

He starts off with 'My girlfriend says ...

How many blokes does it take to change a lightbulb?

Three. One to change it, and two to listen while he brags about how he screwed it ...

How do you know when your **bloke** is getting **old**?

When he starts having dry dreams and wet farts.

How many blokes does it take to change a lightbulb?

One. He just holds it there and waits for the world to revolve around him.

How does a **bloke** take a **bubble bath**?

He eats beans for dinner.

How does a bloke's mind work?
It doesn't ... it's always on sick leave!

How do you know when a bloke is lying?

His lips move.

How is a bloke like the weather?

Nothing can be done to change either one of them.

How can you **tell** if a **bloke** is **excited**?

He's breathing.

How can you grow your own dope?

Bury a bloke and wait till spring.

How does a **bloke** get air to his **brain**?

He opens his flies.

How many blokes does it take to pop popcorn?

Three. One to hold the pan and two others to show off and shake the stove.

How does a **bloke** keep a **woman screaming** after **climax**?

He wipes his willy on the curtains!

How can you find a committed bloke?

Look in a mental institution.

How many **divorced blokes** does it **take** to change a **lightbulb**?

Nobody knows, they never get the house!

How do blokes extend the washing life of their boxer shorts?

They turn them inside out.

How should you **reply** to a **bloke** who says: '**Hey, you're just my type**.'?

'I think you must be mistaken – I have a pulse.'

How do you stop a lust-filled bloke?

Marry him.

How can a bloke tell when a woman has had a good orgasm?

When the buzzing of her vibrator stops.

How could you **spot the blokes** who **stole** a job lot of **Viagra**?

They're a bunch of hardened criminals in

possession of swollen goods.

How many honest, caring, intelligent blokes does it take to do the washing-up?

Both of them.

How do you know if a **bloke's** been in your **garden**?

Your bins have been knocked over and your

dog is pregnant.

How can you **spot a man** with **five willies**?

His underpants fit like a glove!

How do **blokes exercise** on the **beach**?

By sucking in their stomach every time a bikini goes by.

21

GREAT MYSTERIES OF OUR TIME (VII) – WHY?

Why do **blokes** get **married**?

So they don't have to hold their stomachs in anymore.

Why did the **bloke** put **Viagra** in his eyes?
He wanted to look hard.

Why do women need blokes?
Because vibrators can't get a round of drinks in.

Why do **blokes** like **smart women**?
Opposites attract.

Why do blokes keep empty milk bottles in the fridge?
In case anyone wants their coffee black.

Why do **blokes** have **legs**?
So their brains don't drag on the floor.

Why do blokes whistle when they're sitting on the toilet?
So they can remember which end to wipe.

Why is **Santa** such a **happy bloke**?

Because he knows where all the bad girls live.

Why do blokes want to marry virgins?

Because they can't stand criticism.

Why can't **blokes** make **ice cubes**?

They don't know the recipe.

Why do blokes propose?

Because they can't afford our wages!

Why do **little boys** whine?

Because they're practising to be blokes.

Why was Colonel Sanders a typical bloke?

All he cared about were legs, breasts and thighs.

Why do **blokes** need **instant replay** on **TV sports**?

Because after 30 seconds they forget what happened.

Why are bankers good lovers?

They know the penalty for early withdrawals.

Why did the **bloke** cross the **road**?

God knows, why do they bother doing anything?

Why did the **bloke** ask all his **friends** to **save** their **burnt-out** light bulbs?

Because he was trying to build a darkroom.

Why does a **penis** have a **hole** in the **end**?

So blokes can be open-minded.

Why does it snow at Christmas?

Because Santa's coming.

Why shouldn't you hit a bloke with glasses?

A baseball bat is much more effective.

Why did the **stupid bloke** get a **stabbing pain** in his **eye** every time he drank a **cup of tea**?

He forgot to take the spoon out.

Why should you **never** try to find a bloke's **inner child**?
Because you'll have enough trouble coping with his outer one.

Why were blokes given larger brains than dogs?
So they wouldn't hump women's legs at cocktail parties.

Why don't **single** women **fart**?
Because they don't get a bum till they're married.

Why are **women** more **intelligent** than blokes?

Because diamonds are a girl's best friend ... while man's best friend is a dog.

Why does it take **one million** sperm to **fertilise** just **one egg**?
Because they come from a bloke, so they won't stop to ask for directions.

Why did God put blokes' sexual organs on the outside?
So they remember where they are.

Why don't women have blokes' brains?

Because they don't have penises to keep them in.

Why do men like to make salads?

Because they're born tossers.

22

EVERYONE LIKES A LIST, DON'T THEY? (III)

New Training Courses For Men

- Introduction To Common Household Objects I: The Mop.
- Introduction To Common Household Objects II: The Iron.
- Fridge Forensics: Identifying And Removing The Dead.

- Design Pattern Or Splatter Stain On The Lino?:
  You CAN Tell The Difference!
- Accepting Loss I: If It's Empty, You Can Throw It Away.
- Accepting Loss II: If The Milk Expired Three Weeks Ago,
  Keeping It In The Fridge Won't Bring It Back.
- Recycling Skills I: Boxes That The Electronics Came In.
- Recycling Skills II: Polystyrene That Came In The Boxes
  That The Electronics Came In.
- Bathroom Etiquette I: How To Remove Shaving Stubble
  From The Sink.
- Bathroom Etiquette II: Let's Wash Those Towels!

, er ...

- Bathroom Etiquette III: Five Easy Ways To Tell When
  You're About To Run Out Of Toilet Paper!
- Retro? Or Just Hideous?: Re-examining Your '80s Lairy Shirts.
- No, The Dishes Won't Wash Themselves:
  Knowing The Limitations Of Your Kitchenware.
- Going Out To Dinner: Beyond Pizza Hut.
- Expand Your Entertainment Options: Renting Videos That Don't
  Fall Into The 'Action/Adventure' Category.
- Yours, Mine And Ours: Sharing The Remote.
- Adventures In Housekeeping I: Let's Clean The Toilet.

- Adventures In Housekeeping II: Let's Clean Under The Bed.
- Listening: It's Not Just Something You Do During Half-Time.
- Accepting Your Limitations: Just Because You Have Power Tools Doesn't Mean You Can Fix It.

Ten Things Blokes Know About Women:

1.
2.
3.
4.
5.
6.
7.
8.
9.
10. They have tits.

More Harsh Things A Woman Can Say To A Naked Bloke . . .

- Ahhhh, it's cute.
- Make it dance.
- Can I paint a smiley face on it?
- It's OK, we'll work around it.
- Will it squeak if I squeeze it?
- Oh no . . . a flash headache.
- (Giggle and point)
- Can I be honest with you?
- How sweet, you brought incense.
- That explains your car.
- At least this won't take long.
- It looks so unused.
- Why don't we skip right to the cigarettes?
- If you get me really drunk first.
- Is that an optical illusion?
- What *is* that?
- It's a good thing you have so many other talents.
- Does it come with an air pump?
- So this is why you're supposed to judge people on personality.

What Women Want In A Bloke

Original List (Age 22)

1. Handsome.
2. Charming.
3. Financially successful.
4. A caring listener.
5. Witty.
6. In good shape.
7. Dresses with style.
8. Appreciates the finer things.
9. Full of thoughtful surprises.
10. An imaginative, romantic lover.

Revised List (Age 32)

1. Nice-looking – preferably with hair on his head.
2. Opens car doors, pulls out chairs.
3. Has enough money for a nice dinner at a restaurant.
4. Listens more than he talks.
5. Laughs at my jokes at appropriate times.
6. Can carry in all groceries with ease.
7. Owns at least one tie.
8. Appreciates a good home-cooked meal.
9. Remembers birthdays and anniversaries.
10. Seeks romance at least once a week.

Revised List (Age 42)

1. Not too ugly – bald head OK.
2. Doesn't drive off until I'm in the car.
3. Works steadily – splurges on dinner at McDonald's on occasion.
4. Nods head at appropriate times when I'm talking.
5. Usually remembers the punchlines of jokes.
6. Is in good enough shape to rearrange furniture.
7. Usually wears shirt that covers stomach.
8. Knows not to buy champagne with screw-top lids.
9. Remembers to put the toilet seat lid down.
10. Shaves on most weekends.

Revised List (Age 52)

1. Keeps hair in nose and ears trimmed to appropriate length.
2. Doesn't belch or scratch in public.
3. Doesn't borrow money too often.
4. Doesn't nod off to sleep while I'm talking.
5. Doesn't re-tell the same jokes too many times.
6. Is in good enough shape to get off couch on weekends.
7. Usually wears matching socks and fresh underwear.
8. Appreciates a good TV dinner.
9. Remembers your name on occasion.
10. Shaves on some weekends.

Revised List (Age 62)

1. Doesn't scare small children.
2. Remembers where bathroom is.
3. Doesn't require much money for upkeep.
4. Only snores lightly when awake (LOUDLY when asleep).
5. Doesn't forget why he's laughing.
6. Is in good enough shape to stand up by himself.
7. Usually wears some clothes.
8. Likes soft foods.
9. Remembers where he left his teeth.
10. Remembers when . . .

Revised List (Age 72)

1. Breathing . . .

More Cutting Put-Downs For Blokes Who Really Deserve Them

- 'You know you said you wanted to make love to me really badly – well, you've succeeded!'
- '100,000 sperm and you were the fastest?'
- 'You're depriving some poor village of its idiot.'
- 'Save your breath – you'll need it to blow up the only date you'll get tonight.'
- 'If I throw a stick, will you leave?'
- 'A hard-on doesn't count as personal growth.'
- 'I can't be your type – I'm not inflatable.'

Why Are Blokes Like Computers?

- They're hard to figure out and never have enough memory.
- They're supposed to help you solve your problems, but half the time, they are the problem.
- As soon as you commit to one, you realise that if you'd waited a little longer, you could've had a better model.

Why Are Women Brighter Than Blokes?

- We got off the *Titanic* first.
- We can scare bloke bosses with mysterious gynaecological disorder excuses.
- We don't look like a frog in a blender when dancing.
- We don't have to fart to amuse ourselves.
- If we forget to shave, no-one has to know.
- We can congratulate our team-mate without ever touching her rear.
- We have the ability to dress ourselves.
- We never have to reach down every so often to make sure our privates are still there.

- We can talk to people of the opposite sex
  without having to picture them naked.
- If we marry someone 20 years younger, we're aware
  that we look like an idiot.
- We know that there are times when chocolate really can
  solve all your problems.
- We'll never regret piercing our ears.
- We never ejaculate prematurely.
- We can fully assess a person just by looking at their shoes.
- We can make comments about how stupid blokes are in
  their presence, because they aren't listening anyway.

A Christmas Tree Is Better Than A Bloke Because . . .

A Christmas tree is always erect.

*

Even small ones give satisfaction.

*

A Christmas tree stays up for 12 days and nights.

*

A Christmas tree always looks good – even with the lights on.

*

A Christmas tree is always happy with its size.

*

A Christmas tree has cute balls.

*

A Christmas tree doesn't get mad if you break one of its balls.

*

You can throw a Christmas tree out when it starts looking scruffy.

*

You don't have to put up with a Christmas tree all year.

New Drugs On The Market

Following the success of Viagra, pharmaceutical companies are experimenting with a whole range of drugs designed to improve the performance of blokes in today's society. Here are some of the most promising ...

- **BUYAGRA** – Married and otherwise attached blokes reported a sudden urge to buy their womenfolk expensive jewellery and gifts after taking this drug for just two days. Still to be seen: whether this drug can encourage them to stretch to a new designer wardrobe and an exotic holiday too.

- **COMPLIMENTRA** – In clinical trials, 82 per cent of middle-aged blokes given this drug noticed that their wives had a new hairstyle. Currently being tested to see if its effects can extend to noticing new clothing.

· **FLYAGRA** – This drug is showing special promise in treating blokes with OFD (open-fly disorder). Especially useful for blokes on Viagra.

· **DIRECTRA** – A dose of this drug given to blokes before leaving on car trips caused 72 per cent of them to stop and ask directions when they got lost, compared to a control group of 0.2 per cent.

· **NEGA-SPORTAGRA** – Blokes reported that this drug had the strange effect of making them want to turn off televised sports and actually chat to their girlfriends.

23

IT'S A
BIBLE
THING! (III)

One day in the Garden of Eden, Eve calls out to God: 'Lord, I have a problem.'

'What's the problem, Eve?'

'Lord, I know you've created me and have provided this beautiful garden and all of these wonderful animals, and that hilarious snake, but I'm just not happy.'

'Why is that, Eve?' came the reply from above.

'Lord, I am lonely, and sick of apples.'

'Well, Eve, in that case I have a solution. I shall create a bloke for you.'

'What's a bloke, Lord?'

'This bloke will be a flawed creature, with aggressive tendencies, an enormous ego, and an inability to empathise or listen to you properly. All in all, he'll give you a hard time. But he'll be bigger and faster, and more muscular than you. He'll be really good at fighting and kicking a ball about and hunting, and not all that bad in the sack.'

'Sounds great,' says Eve, with an ironically raised eyebrow.

'Yeah, well, you can have him on one condition,' says God. 'Because of his tender ego, you'll have to let him think I made him first. Just remember, it's our little secret … **You know, woman to woman.'**

A bloke says to God: 'God, why did you make woman so beautiful?'
God says: 'So you would love her.'
'But God,' the bloke says. 'Why did you make her so dumb?'
God says: **'So she would love you.'**

One day three blokes were out walking and came upon a raging, violent river. They needed to get to the other side, but didn't know how.

The first bloke prayed to God, saying: 'Please God, give me the strength to cross this river.'

Poof! God gave him big arms and strong legs, and he was able to swim across the river in about two hours.

Seeing this, the second man prayed to God, saying: 'Please God, give me the strength and ability to cross this river.'

Poof! God gave him a rowing boat and he was able to row across the river in about an hour.

The third man saw how this worked out for the other two, so he also prayed to God, saying: 'Please God, give me the strength, ability and courage to cross this river.'

And poof! God turned him into a woman and he walked across the bridge.

When God created man, she was only joking.

What would have happened if it had been **three Wise Women** instead of **three Wise Men**?

They would have asked directions, arrived on time, helped deliver the baby, cleaned the stable, made a casserole and brought practical gifts.

But what would they have said when they left . . . ?

'Did you see the sandals Mary was wearing with that gown?'

'That baby doesn't look anything like Joseph!'

'Virgin, my arse! I knew her in school!'

'Can you believe they let all of those disgusting animals in the house?'

'I heard Joseph isn't even working right now!'

'And that donkey they're riding has seen better days, too!'

'Want to bet on how long it'll take to get your casserole dish back?'

Why do only 10 per cent of blokes make it to heaven?

Because if they all went, it would be hell.

Ten Reasons God Created Eve

1. God worried that Adam would always be lost in the Garden because blokes hate to ask for directions.

2. God knew that Adam would one day need someone to hand him the TV remote. (Blokes don't want to see what's ON TV, they want to see WHAT ELSE is on!)

3. God knew that Adam would never buy a new fig leaf when his seat wore out and would need Eve to tell him what an arse he was making of himself.

4. God knew that Adam would never make a doctor's appointment for himself.

5. God knew that Adam would never remember when to put the rubbish out for the dustmen.

6. God knew that if the world was to be populated, blokes would never be able to handle childbearing.

7. As 'Keeper of the Garden', Adam would never remember where he put his tools.

8. The scripture account of creation indicates Adam needed someone to blame his troubles on when God caught him hiding in the Garden.

9. As the Bible says: 'It is not good for man to be alone.'

10. When God finished the creation of Adam, He stepped back, scratched His head and said: 'I can do better than that.'

Why did God create alcohol?

So ugly blokes would get the chance to have sex.

One day The Lord spoke to Adam: 'I've got some good news and some bad news.' Adam looked at The Lord and replied: 'Well, give me the good news first.'

Smiling, The Lord explained: 'I've got two new organs for you. One is called a brain and it will allow you to create new things, solve problems and have intelligent conversations with Eve. The other organ I have for you is called a penis. It will give you great physical pleasure and allow you to reproduce your now-intelligent life form and populate this planet. Eve will be very happy that you now have this organ to give her children.'

Adam, very excited, exclaimed: 'These are great gifts you've given to me. What could possibly be bad news after such great tidings?'

The Lord looked upon Adam and said with great sorrow: 'You'll never be able to use these two gifts at the same time.'

24

WHAT'S THE DIFFERENCE, ANYWAY? (II)

What's the **difference** between
a **bloke** and a **Brussels sprout**?
One is tasteless and smells of farts
and the other is a nutritious vegetable!

What's the **difference** between a **bloke** and a **vibrator**?
A vibrator won't make you sleep in the wet patch.

What's the **difference** between **blokes** and **women**?
A woman wants one bloke to satisfy her every need.
A bloke wants every woman to satisfy his one need.

What's the **difference** between a **bloke** and **ET**?
ET phones home.

What's the difference between **blokes** and **women**?

Women dream of world peace, a safe environment and eliminating hunger. Blokes dream of being stuck in a lift with Destiny's Child.

What's the **difference** between a single **bloke** and a **married bloke**?
A single bloke will lie awake all night thinking about something you say. A married bloke will fall asleep before you finish.

What's the difference between a bloke and a bird?
A bird can whistle through its pecker.

What's the difference between **blokes' sex talk** and **women's sex talk**?

When a bloke talks dirty to a woman, it's sexual harassment. When a woman talks dirty to a bloke, it's 49p a minute.

What's the difference between women's relationships with their children and blokes'?

Women know about their children's dentist appointments, football games, romances, best friends, favourite foods, secret fears and hopes and dreams. Blokes are vaguely aware of some short people living in the house.

What's the **difference** between a **bloke** and a **catfish**?

One's a bottom-feeding scum-sucker – the other's a fish!

What's the difference between a woman's behaviour during the menopause and a bloke's?

A menopausal woman goes through a variety of complex emotional, psychological and biological changes that vary from individual to individual. The menopause in men provokes an identical reaction – they all buy Raybans sunglasses and leather driving gloves, then go shopping for a Porsche.

25

WHO SAYS BLOKES HAVE ONE-TRACK MINDS?

A bloke walks up to his wife in the kitchen one morning, pinches her on her bottom and says: 'You know, if you firmed this up, we could get rid of your girdle.'

While this was borderline intolerable, she bit her tongue and stayed silent.

The next morning the bloke wakes his wife with a pinch on the boob and says: 'You know, if you firmed these up, we could get rid of your bra.'

This was beyond a joke, so she rolls over and grabs him by the penis. With a death grip in place, she says: 'You know, if you firmed this up, we could get rid of the postman, the gardener, the odd-job man and your brother.'

D ave walks into the bar and sees his mate Jeff huddled over a table, depressed. Dave walks over and asks Jeff what's wrong. 'Well,' replies Jeff. 'You know that beautiful girl at work I wanted to ask out, but couldn't because I got an erection every time I saw her?'

'Yes,' replies Dave with a smile.

'Well,' says Jeff, straightening up. 'I finally plucked up the courage to ask her out, and she agreed.'

'That's great!' says Dave. 'When's the date?'

'I went to meet her this evening,' continues Jeff. 'But because I was worried I'd get an erection again, I got some sticky tape and taped my todger to my leg, so if I did, it wouldn't show.'

'Sensible,' says Dave.

'So I got to her door,' says Jeff, 'and I rang her doorbell. And she answered it in the sheerest, tiniest dress you ever saw.'

'And what happened then?'

Jeff huddles over the table again.

'I kicked her in the face.'

Three women were having a laugh, comparing their blokes' love techniques to cars:

The first says: 'My lover's like a Rolls Royce ... sophisticated and comfortable.'

The second says: 'Mine is like a Ferrari ... fast and powerful.'

The third says: 'Well, my lover's like an old Morris Minor ... you have to start him by hand and jump on when he gets going.'

A bloke is sitting next to a gorgeous woman on a plane. He strikes up a conversation, but then she asks if he minds her reading her book.

Bloke: 'No, not at all! What are you reading?'

Woman: '*The Joy Of Sex*.'

Bloke: 'Hmm. Anything interesting?'

Woman: 'Yeah. Apparently, a man's nationality can indicate things about his penis size.'

Bloke: 'OK, like what?'

Woman: 'Well, Polish men have the longest ones and American Indians have the thickest. Oh, by the way, my name is Laura Smith.'

Bloke: 'Nice to meet you, Laura. My name's Tonto Kawalski.'

A bloke and his wife have separate bedrooms because of his loud snoring. One night when he's feeling amorous, the bloke calls out to his wife. 'Oh, my little boopey-boo, I miss you.'

So his wife gets up and goes to his room, but as she's walking in, she trips on the carpet and falls flat on her face.

'Oh,' he says sweetly. 'Did my little honey-woney hurt her ickle nosey-wosey?'

The woman picks herself up, gets in her husband's bed and they make passionate love.

Afterwards, as she's going back to her room, she once again trips on the carpet and falls flat on her face.

The bloke raises his head from the pillow, looks at his wife lying on the floor and says:

'Clumsy bitch.'

A really good-looking bloke walks into a singles bar, gets a drink and takes a seat. During the course of the evening he tries to chat up every single woman who walks into the bar, with no luck. Suddenly a real pig of a bloke walks in. He sits at the bar, and within seconds he's surrounded by women. Very soon he walks out of the bar with two of the most beautiful women you ever saw. Disheartened by all this, the good-looking bloke goes up to the barman and says: 'Excuse me, but that minging bloke just came in here and left with those two stunning women – what's his secret? He's as ugly as sin and I'm everything a girl could want.' 'Well,' says the barman. 'I don't know how he does it, but the same thing happens every night. He walks in, orders a drink, and just sits there licking his eyebrows . . . '

A bloke is walking through a hotel lobby when he accidentally bumps into a woman and his elbow digs into her breast. 'Oh, sorry,' he says. 'But if your heart is as soft as your breast, I know you'll forgive me.' And the woman replies: 'And if your penis is as hard as your elbow, I'm in Room 103!!!'

The blind date didn't go well, but as the woman arrives at her door, relieved that the evening is finally over, the bloke suddenly says: 'Do you want to see my underwear?'

Before she can respond, he drops his trousers, right there in the hall, revealing that he isn't wearing any underwear. She glances down and says:

'Nice design
– does it also come
in men's sizes?'

Two women are having a conversation about their blokes when the first one says: 'My bloke said he fantasised about having two girls at once.'
The other replies: 'Yeah, most blokes do. What did you tell him?'
'I said, "If you can't satisfy one woman, why would you want to piss off two?"'

A young bloke is sitting next to an old priest on a plane, waiting for take-off. There's a minor technical hitch delaying things so the Captain announces that the airline will be serving a round of free drinks. When the lovely air hostess comes by for their order, the bloke asks for a double Scotch. She then asks the priest if he'd like a drink. 'Oh no,' says the priest. 'I'd rather commit adultery than drink alcohol.' Stopping in mid-swallow and dribbling Scotch down his front, the bloke replaces his drink on the hostess's drinks cart. 'Excuse me, miss,' he says. 'I didn't know I had a choice!'

A bloke's sitting in a cinema, and when the usherette asks to see his ticket, he flashes at her. Unfazed, she says:

'I asked to see your ticket

– not your stub!'

A bloke and his girlfriend are just about to have sex when she asks if he's got a condom.
'Of course,' the bloke replies. 'In fact, I bought a special Olympic pack with gold, silver and bronze-coloured ones.' As he starts to put on the gold one, his girlfriend stops him and says: 'Could you put the silver one on?' When the bloke asks why, she replies: 'So you come second for a change!'

Tell this one to a bloke to wind him up ...

Have you heard that women's orgasms can be categorised into one of four types? They are the Positive Orgasm, the Negative Orgasm, the Holy Orgasm and the Fake Orgasm.

It's really easy to identify them, too:

When having a Positive Orgasm, a woman will cry:

'Oh yes, oh yes ... oh yes!'

When having a Negative Orgasm, a woman will cry:

'Oh no, no ... oh no!'

When having a Holy Orgasm, she'll cry:

'Oh God, oh God ... oh, God!'

When having a Fake Orgasm, she'll cry:

'Oh Paul, oh Paul ... oh Paul*!'

NB * Substitute bloke's name with the name of the bloke you're telling the joke to.

26

GREAT MYSTERIES OF OUR TIME (VIII) – HOW COME?

How do blokes sort their laundry?

'Filthy' and 'filthy, but wearable'.

How does a bloke keep his youth?

By giving her money, diamonds and designer clothes.

How many **blokes** does it take to **change** a **light bulb**?

Two – one to change the bulb and one to collect the medal.

How do you stop a bloke biting his nails?

Make him wear shoes.

How many blokes does it take to put the
toilet seat down?

Nobody knows. It hasn't happened yet.

How do you **stop** a **bloke** breaking into your **house**?

Replace all the locks with bra fasteners.

How do you get a bloke to climb up on the roof?

You tell him the drinks are on the house.

How do you **confuse** a **bloke**?

You don't, they're just born that way.

How many blokes does it take to change a light bulb?

Three – one to screw in the bulb, and two to listen to him brag
about the screwing part.

How do you **start** a **conversation** with a **bloke** in a **flower shop**?

'So, what did you do?'

How do you stop blokes from spitting?

Turn down the grill.

How do you reply to a bloke who says: 'I knew that!
I'm not a complete idiot, you know!'
'Oh! What part is missing then?'

How do you **kill** a **bloke**?
Ask him to jump off his ego and land on his IQ.

How many blokes does it take to change a light bulb?
As many as you like – it'll still be there waiting to be changed
in the morning.

How do you stop your **bloke** reading your **email**?
Rename the mail folder 'instruction manuals'.

How do you spot the most popular bloke at the nudist colony?
He's the one who can have a cup of coffee in each
hand and still carry a dozen doughnuts.

How do you know when a bloke's had an orgasm?
He snores.

How do you **make** a **bloke** scream when you are having **sex**?

Phone him.

How many men does it take to change a light bulb?

None, they just sit there in the dark and complain.

How do we know **blokes** invented **maps**?

Who else would turn an inch into a mile?

How can you spot a blind bloke at a nudist colony?

It isn't hard.

How many **men** does it take to **change** a **light bulb**?

None. They're happy living in the shadows.

How many bloke jokes are there?

None, they're all true.

27

DOCTOR, DOCTOR…(II)

A bloke goes to the doctor's and complains that he can't do all the things around the house that he used to do. When the examination is complete, the bloke says: 'C'mon, Doc, I can take it. Tell me in plain English what's wrong with me.'

'Well, in plain English,' replies the doctor, 'you're just lazy.'

'OK,' says the bloke. 'Now give me the medical term for it so I can tell my wife.'

A bloke hasn't been feeling well so he goes for a complete check-up. Afterwards the doctor comes out with the results ...

'I'm afraid I have some very bad news,' says the doctor. 'You're dying, and you don't have much time left.'

'That's terrible,' says the bloke. 'How long have I got?'

'Ten,' the doctor says, sadly.

'Ten?' the bloke asks. 'Ten what? Months? Weeks? What?'

'Nine ... Eight ...'

A bloke goes to the doctor's and says: 'Doctor, I have an embarrassing sexual problem. I can't get it up for my wife any more.'

'Bring her in tomorrow,' says the doctor. 'Then I'll see what I can do.'

The following day the bloke returns with his wife. The doctor asks her to remove her clothes, turn all the way round, then lie down on the examining table. After asking her to get dressed again, he takes the bloke to one side and says: 'It's OK, you're in perfect health. Your wife doesn't give me an erection either!'

A bloke goes to see a psychiatrist wearing only clingfilm for shorts. The shrink says: **'Well, I can clearly see you're nuts.'**

A bloke goes to the doctor's because he's having problems getting an erection. After a complete examination the doctor tells him that the muscles around the base of his penis were damaged from a prior viral infection and the only option is an experimental treatment, if he were willing to take the risk. The treatment consists of implanting muscle tissue from an elephant's trunk in the bloke's penis.

The bloke thinks about it for a while. The idea of going through life without ever experiencing sex again is too much for him to bear. So, with the assurance that there would be no cruelty to the elephant, the bloke decides to go for it.

A few weeks after the operation, he's given the green light to use his newly renovated equipment so he plans a romantic evening with his girlfriend in one of the nicest restaurants in town.

However, half way through dinner he feels a stirring between his legs that continues to the point of being extremely painful. To release the pressure, he unzips his flies – and immediately his penis springs from his pants, goes to the top of the table, grabs a roll, then returns to his pants.

His girlfriend is stunned at first, but then with a sly smile on her face, says: 'That was incredible. Can you do it again?'

With his eyes watering, the bloke replies:

'I think I can, but I'm not sure if I can fit another roll up my arse.'

A family gather in a hospital waiting room where their relative lies gravely ill. Finally, the doctor comes in looking tired and sombre. 'I'm afraid I'm the bearer of bad news,' he says as he surveys the worried faces. 'The only hope left for your loved one at this time is a brain transplant. It's an experimental procedure, semi-risky and you'll have to pay for the brain yourselves.' The family members sit silent as they absorb the news. After a great length of time, someone asks: 'Well, how much does a brain cost?' The doctor quickly responds: '£5,000 for a bloke's brain, and £200 for a woman's brain.' The moment turns awkward. The men in the room try not to smile, avoiding eye contact with the women, but some actually smirk. One bloke, unable to control his curiosity, blurts out the question everyone wants to ask: 'Why is the bloke's brain so much more expensive?' The doctor smiles at his childish innocence and says: 'It's just standard pricing procedure. We have to mark down the price of the women's brains because they've actually been used.'

A bloke goes to the doctor's with a flywheel between his legs. The doctor asks: 'What's that?' And the bloke replies: 'I don't know, but it's driving me nuts!'

An 80-year-old bloke is having his annual check-up, and when the doctor asks him how he's feeling, he replies: 'I've never been better! I've got an 18-year-old bride who's pregnant with my child! What do you think about that?'

The doctor considers this for a moment, then says: 'Well, let me tell you a story. I know a bloke who's an avid hunter. He never misses a season. But one day he's in a bit of a hurry and he accidentally grabs his umbrella instead of his gun. So he's walking in the woods near a creek and suddenly spots a beaver in some brush in front of him! He raises up his umbrella, points it at the beaver and squeezes the handle. BAM!!! The beaver drops dead in front of him.'

'That's impossible!' says the old bloke in disbelief. 'Someone else must have shot that beaver.'

'My point, exactly.'

A bloke goes to see the doctor after a sudden illness. He takes his wife with him and after a thorough examination the doctor asks if he could speak to the wife for a moment. The bloke leaves the room while the doctor tells the wife the bad news. 'Your husband has a rare condition – any form of stress could instantly kill him so you must cater to his every whim. Make him breakfast, lunch and dinner. Make love to him whenever he requires. Don't give him any bad news at all. Is that understood?' The wife nods and then leaves to join her husband. Once outside, the bloke asks his wife: 'What did the doctor say?' She replies solemnly:

'He said you're going to die very soon.'

One day Paul complained to his mate, Simon: 'Blimey, my elbow really hurts. Do you think I should go and see a doctor?'

'No,' says Simon. 'There's a computer at the chemist's down the road that can diagnose anything far quicker than a doctor, just by analysing your urine. And it only costs a fiver.'

Paul figures he has nothing to lose so he wees into a jar and takes it to the chemist's. After he's put the sample and a fiver into the machine, it grinds into action and then spits out a small slip of paper, which reads: 'You have tennis elbow. Soak your arm in warm water. Avoid heavy work. It'll be better in two weeks.'

That evening, while thinking about how amazing this new technology is, Paul began to wonder whether the computer could be fooled. He decided to give it a try. He mixed up some tap water, a stool sample from his dog, urine samples from his wife and daughter, and to top it off, he masturbated into the concoction. He went back to the chemist's and, giggling, put the sample and a fiver into the computer. It made the usual noises, then spat out a slip of paper, which read: 'Your tap water is too hard – get a water softener. Your dog has ringworm – bathe him in anti-fungal shampoo. Your daughter is using cocaine – put her in a rehab clinic. Your wife is pregnant with twin girls. They're not yours – get a lawyer. And if you don't stop wanking, your tennis elbow will never get better!'

He He He .

A bloke goes to the doctor's because he's been sunbathing too long and has got badly burnt.

'Yes,' says the doctor, after examining the bloke's whole body. 'It's definitely severe sunburn. I'll write you a prescription.'

Checking to see what the doctor had prescribed, the bloke was surprised that he'd written down calamine lotion and Viagra.

'That's odd,' says the bloke. 'I can see the need for the calamine lotion, but why the Viagra?'

And the doctor replies:

'That's to keep the sheets off you at night.'

A middle-aged bloke has a heart attack and while on the operating table he has a near-death experience. He sees God and asks if this is it. God says: 'No. You've got another 30 to 40 years left to live.'

When the bloke recovers he decides to stay in the hospital and have a face-lift, tummy tuck and hair implants, figuring that if he's got that long he may as well make the most of it.

Then, when he walks out of the hospital after the last operation he immediately gets hit by an ambulance. Arriving before God again, he says: 'I thought you said I'd got another 30 to 40 years.' To which God replies:

'To tell you the truth, I didn't recognise you!'

28

WHAT ARE THEY LIKE?! (III)

Why are blokes like old bras?
They hang around your boobs all day and
give you no support when it's needed.

Why are blokes like photo-copiers?

You need them for reproduction, but that's about it.

Why are **blokes** like **textbooks**?

You have to spend a lot of time between the covers to gain a small amount of satisfaction.

Why are blokes like crystal?

Some look really good, but you can still see right through them.

Why are **blokes** like **lawnmowers**?

They're hard to get started, they emit noxious odours and half the time they don't work.

Why are blokes like fine wine?

They all start out like grapes, and it's our job to stomp on them and keep them in the dark until they mature into something you'd like to have dinner with.

Why are **blokes** like **newborn** babies?

They're cute at first, but pretty soon you get tired of cleaning up their crap.

Why are blokes like curling tongs?

They're always hot and in your hair.

Why are **blokes** like **adverts**?

You can't believe a word they say.

Why are blokes like miniskirts?

If you're not careful, they'll creep up your legs.

Why are blokes like microwave meals?

They're both finished in 30 seconds.

Why are **blokes** like **bananas**?
The older they get, the less firm they are.

Why are **sensitive blokes** like **UFOs**?
You often hear about them, but you never see one.

Why are **blokes** like the **weather**?
You can't do anything to change either of them.

Why are **blokes** like **government bonds**?
Because they take so long to mature.

Why are **blokes** like **tights**?
They either cling, run or don't fit right in the crotch!

Why are **blokes** like **dogs**?

They're smelly, constantly demand food and are both afraid of vacuum cleaners.

29

SO THIS BLOKE GOES INTO A PUB...(III)

A bloke's in the pub and decides he'd better go home, hoping he can manage to get back early enough so as not to piss his wife off for drinking after work. When he gets home, though, he finds her in bed with his boss. Later, back in the pub, he tells the barman what's just happened. 'That's awful,' says the barman. 'What did you do?'

'Well, I carefully sneaked back out the door and came back here. I mean, they were only just starting so I figured I had time for a couple more pints!'

Two blokes go on holiday together, and while Sam always has great success with the ladies, Ken gets nowhere.

'How can I impress the women like you do?' asks Ken. Sam gives him a potato, telling him that if he puts it in his trunks he can't fail. But after an hour of parading up and down the beach Ken gets disillusioned because he still hasn't pulled. 'It's no good, the potato trick hasn't worked,' says Ken in a sulk. Sam can barely contain his laughter when he spots the problem: 'No, you were meant to put it down the FRONT of your trunks!'

Two aliens are circling Earth, discussing its inhabitants. 'So what do you think? Intelligent life or not?' asks the first alien.

And the second answers: 'Hmm, the ones with the brains seem to be OK, but I'm not so sure about the ones with the balls!'

Gary asks John to help him mend his car after work, so they go back to Gary's place to get going in the garage. But before they start, Gary goes up to his wife, kisses her, tells her she's beautiful and how much he's missed her while he was out at work. When suppertime comes he compliments her on the meal she's cooked and tells her he loves her. Back in the garage later, John mentions his surprise at how attentive Gary is to his wife. Gary says that he started behaving like this a few months before and that it had really perked up their marriage.

John thinks it's got to be worth a try so when he gets home he gives his wife a massive hug, kisses her and tells her he loves her, but she just bursts into tears. John's confused and asks her why she's crying. 'This is the worst day of my life,' she says. 'First, little Jack fell off his bike and twisted his ankle, then the washing machine broke and flooded the kitchen. And now you come home drunk!'

A blond bloke, wanting to earn some money, decides to hire himself out as a handyman-type and starts canvassing a wealthy neighbourhood. He goes to the front door of the first house and asks the owner if she has any odd jobs. 'Well, how much would you charge to paint my porch?' she asks.

The blond bloke replies: 'How about £50?' and she agrees, telling him that the paint and other materials he might need are in the garage.

The woman's husband, inside the house, hears the conversation and says to his wife: 'Does he realise the porch goes all the way around the house?' To which she replies: 'He should, he was standing on it.'

A short time later, the blond bloke comes to the door to collect his money. 'You're finished already?' she asks. 'Yes,' he answers. 'And I had paint left over, so I gave it two coats.' Impressed, the woman reaches in her purse for the £50.

'And by the way,' the blond bloke adds.

'It's not a Porsche, it's a Ferrari!'

A fat bloke sees a notice in a shop window: 'A bed, a woman and a pie for £5.'

He goes into the shop and says to the owner: 'Is that right – a bed, a woman and a pie for only £5?'

'Of course,' says the shopkeeper.

'Sounds like a bargain, but what kind of pies are they?' asks the fat bloke.

This bloke walks into a bar and says: 'OUCH! Who put that there?'

This bloke goes to the Cup Final and notices that there's an empty seat between him and the next spectator. 'Imagine that,' he comments. 'Someone had a ticket for the most important game of the year and didn't turn up.' The guy next to him explains that the seat was for his wife, that every year they went to the final together, but she had died now and this was the first time he'd come on his own. 'That's awful!' says the first guy. 'Couldn't you have got a friend or relative to come with you?'

'No,' he replies. 'Everyone I know is at her funeral.'

A bloke goes before a judge to try to get excused from jury service, and the judge asks him why he can't serve as a juror. 'I don't want to be away from my job for that long,' replies the bloke.

'Can't they do without you at work?' asks the judge.

'Yes,' says the bloke. 'But I don't want them to know it.'

A bloke goes to Las Vegas on a gambling holiday that goes really badly for him. He loses everything except a dollar and the return air ticket, but knows if he can just get to the airport, he can get home. Outside the casino is a cab, so the bloke explains his situation to the cabbie. He promises to send the money from home, gives his address, his passport number, everything, but the cabbie just answers: 'If you don't have the $15 fare, get out of my cab!' so the poor bloke has to hitch-hike to the airport and only just catches his flight in time.

A year later, having worked really hard to build up his finances again, the bloke goes back to Vegas, figuring that this time he has to win. And he does – big time! When he leaves the casino to go back to the airport, he sees the miserable cabbie at the end of a long line of taxis and plans his revenge.

He gets into the first taxi in the queue and asks how much to go to the airport. 'Fifteen dollars,' comes the reply. 'And how much for you to give me a blow job on the way?' he asks. 'Get out of my cab!' screams the cabbie.

The bloke gets into the back of every taxi in the long queue and asks the same question, getting exactly the same reply from every cabbie. But when he gets to the cab of his old enemy, he just asks: 'How much to the airport?' Then, when the old cabbie says, 'Fifteen dollars,' he says, 'OK.'

Then, as they drive past the long line of cabs, the bloke gives a big smile and a thumbs-up to the rest of the cabbies.

A bloke gets a job working on a round-the-world cruise liner. At every port he sends his granny a beach photograph of himself, but one of the destinations was a nudist beach. He decides to have his picture taken anyway and cuts it in half. Two days later he's horrified when he realises he's sent his gran the wrong half of the photo,
so he gets on the phone to try and explain what's happened.

'Gran, did you get my last photograph?' he asks.
'Yes, dear,' she says.

'But I think you should change your hairstyle – this one makes your nose look really big.'

Drugs Alert – Please Be Aware. Bloke Date Rape Drug

Police warn all blokes who are regular clubbers, party-goers and unsuspecting public-house regulars to be more alert and cautious when getting a drink offer from a girl. There is a drug called beer, which is essentially in liquid form. The drug is now being used by female sexual predators at parties to convince their male victims to have sex with them. The shocking statistic is that beer is available virtually anywhere!

All girls have to do is buy a beer or two for almost any bloke and simply ask him home for no-strings-attached sex. Blokes are literally rendered helpless against such attacks, which generally come from otherwise unattractive women who render their prey legless in order have their evil way. Please! Warn every bloke you know ...

However, if you fall victim to this deceptive drug and the crooked women who are handing them out, there are male support groups with venues in every area, where you can discuss the details of your shocking encounter in an open and frank manner with a bunch of similarly affected, like-minded blokes.

For your nearest venue, simply look up 'Pub' in the *Yellow Pages*.

One night a woman finds her husband standing over their newborn baby's crib. Silently she watches him as the bloke's expression reveals disbelief, delight, amazement, scepticism and enchantment. Touched by this unusual display of deep emotion, she slips her arms round her husband. 'A penny for your thoughts,' she asks.

'It's amazing,' the bloke replies. 'I just can't see how anyone can make a cot like that for only £46.50.'

A bloke's in a quandary because he has to get rid of one of his staff. He's narrowed it down to one of two people, Debra or Jack, but it's a hard decision as they're both equally qualified and both do excellent work.

He finally decides that in the morning whichever one uses the water cooler first will have to go.

Debra comes in the next morning, hugely hung-over after partying all night. As she goes to the cooler to get some water to take an aspirin, the bloke approaches her and says: 'Debra, I've never done this before, but I have to lay you or Jack off.'

err . . . .

Debra replies:

**'Could you jack
off, I've got a
terrible headache.'**

A woman goes to buy her boyfriend a pet for his birthday, but finds most of the ones in the shop too expensive, so she asks the shop assistant for advice.

'Well,' he said. 'I've got a large bullfrog going cheap, and they say it's been trained to give blow jobs. I can't prove it, but we have been selling a lot of them.'

The woman figures this would be a great joke gift anyway. And if it did give blow jobs, she'd never have to face them herself again.

When she gives her bloke the frog, she tells him about its supposed special skill and while he doesn't fall for it either, they have a good giggle about it and go to bed. In the middle of the night, though, she's woken up by the noise of pots and pans flying about downstairs in the kitchen. As she goes to investigate, she finds her bloke and the frog reading cookbooks.

'What are you two doing at this hour?' she asks. And the bloke replies:

'If I can teach this frog to cook, you're outta here!'

30

GREAT MYSTERIES OF OUR TIME (IX) – WHAT'S ALL THAT ABOUT?

What's a bloke's idea of honesty in a relationship?
Telling you his real name.

What's a **bloke's** idea of **foreplay**?
Watching the end of the match first.

What do blokes use for birth control?

Their personalities.

What do you call that insensitive bit at the base of the penis?
A bloke.

What's the **fastest** way to a **bloke's** heart?
Through his chest with a sharp implement.

What do you call a bloke who says he's in touch with his feminine side?

A liar!

What should you give a bloke who has everything?

A woman to show him how to work it.

What's the best way to kill a bloke?

**Put a naked woman and a six-pack
in front of him.
Then tell him to pick just one.**

What do you say to a bloke if he asks
you whether you fancy a quickie?
'As opposed to what?'

What do you call a **bloke**
with a **small willy**?
Justin ...

What do single blokes have if mums have Mother's Day
and dads have Father's Day?
Palm Sunday.

What's the **definition**
of **mixed emotions**?
Watching the bloke who just dumped
you crash into your spanking new car.

What should you do with your bum before having sex?
Drop him off at the golf club.

What happens when a vain and irritating bloke takes Viagra?

He gets taller.

What do you call a **man** who does the **washing up**, cleaning and is always **polite** and **helpful**?

A wo-man.

What do you call a **bloke** with a **big willy** and **lots of cash**?

Darling.

What is six-inches long, three-inches wide
and drives women wild?

A £50 note!

What do you call a **bloke** with an **IQ** of **five**?
Gifted.

What does it mean when a bloke is in your bed, gasping
for breath and calling your name?

You didn't hold the pillow down long enough.

What do you call a **woman**
with half a **brain cell**?

A bloke.

What do you call a **zit** on
a **bloke's penis**?

A brain tumour.

What do you call a fly in a bloke's brain?

Space invader.

What should you say to a bloke whose chat-up line is: 'Do you want to come home and sit on my face?'

'Why, is your nose bigger than your penis?'

What should you do if you see your ex-boyfriend rolling around in pain on the ground?
Shoot him again.

What did the elephant say to the naked bloke?

How do you drink with that?

What's more useful –
a **bloke** or a **chocolate fireguard**?
Well, a chocolate fireguard can
make a lovely sauce.

What's got eight arms and an IQ of 60?

**Four blokes watching
a football game.**

What do you call a **bunch of blokes** in a **circle**?

A dope ring.

What's the definition of a male chauvinist pig?

A bloke who hates every bone in a woman's body, except his own.

What's a **bloke's** idea of **romance**?

You go and fetch him another can after sex.

What makes blokes **chase women** they have **no** intention of **marrying**? The same urge that makes dogs chase cars they have no intention of driving.

What's the definition of a bloke?

A vibrator with a wallet!

What did the **elephant** say to the **bloke**? 'It's cute, but can you pick up peanuts with it?!'

What's the best form of birth control for a bloke over 50?

Nudity.

31

WOMEN ON TOP (II)

A bloke's at his wedding rehearsal and decides he wants to start married life with the upper hand. He takes the vicar aside and says: 'Look, I'll give you £100 if you'll change the wedding vows. Can you leave in the "love, honour and obey" bit and take out "forsaking all others, be faithful only unto her"?' The bloke then passes the vicar the cash and walks away smugly.

The day of the wedding arrives and when it comes to the groom's vows, the vicar looks him straight in the eye and says: 'Will you promise to prostrate yourself before her, obey her every command and wish, serve her breakfast in bed every morning of your life and swear eternally before God and your lovely wife that you will never even look at another women, as long as you both shall live?'

The groom gulps and looks around, then says in a tiny voice: 'I will.'

After the service the furious groom takes the vicar aside again and hisses: 'I thought we had a deal!'

The vicar gives him back his £100 and whispers back: 'She made me a much better offer.'

A bloke steps on to one of those speak-your-weight machines that also tell your fortune.

'Listen to this,' he tells his wife, showing her a small white card. 'It says I'm energetic, bright, resourceful and a great lover.'

'Yes,' his wife nods. **'And it's got your weight wrong, too!'**

Two women are sitting on a park bench, when along comes a bloke.

Women: 'We bet you that we can guess your age!'

Bloke: 'Go on then! Bet you can't.'

Women: 'OK – we need you to take your trousers down!'

Bloke: 'Errrrr, OK.'

Women: 'And now we need you to take your pants down!'

Bloke: 'What? Er, OK then.'

Women: 'You're 27!'

Bloke: 'WOW! Amazing! I am 27 – you could tell that just by looking at my bits?'

Women: 'No, you told us yesterday.'

A boring bloke
says to his wife:
'Honey, why
are you wearing
your wedding
ring on the
wrong finger?'

**And the bored wife replies:
'Because I married the wrong man!'**

Ten blokes and one woman are hanging on to a rope beneath a helicopter. They know there are too many on the rope and that if someone doesn't get off, the rope will break and they'll all die, but they can't decide who should make the sacrifice. Finally, the woman gives a really touching speech, saying how she'll give up her life to save the others because women are used to giving up things for their husbands and children, offering themselves to blokes and not receiving anything in return. When she finishes speaking, all the blokes applaud her bravery.

Proving that blokes should never underestimate the intelligence of a woman.

A woman finds an old lamp in the attic and when she polishes it, a genie pops out and offers to grant her three wishes. However, he warns her that whatever she wishes for, the bloke in her life will get ten times better or more. So the woman thinks about this and says: 'For my first wish, I'd like to be the most beautiful woman in the world.' The genie says: 'OK, but remember your bloke will be the most handsome man in the world and every woman will lust after him.' The woman replies: 'Go ahead.' So sure enough, she's the world's most beautiful woman. 'For my second wish, I want to be the richest woman in the world.' The genie warns: 'That will make your bloke ten times richer than you.' 'Fine by me,' is the reply. So she's the richest woman in the world. The genie asks: 'What is your final wish?' Her reply: 'I'd like a very mild heart attack!'

A bloke is sitting quietly reading his paper one morning when his wife sneaks up behind him and whacks him on the back of his head with a huge frying pan.

Bloke: 'What was that for?'

Wife: 'What was that piece of paper in your jacket pocket with the name "Marianne" written on it?'

Bloke: 'Remember two weeks ago when I went to the races? "Marianne" was the name of one of the horses I bet on.'

The wife looks sheepish, apologises and goes to put the frying pan back in the kitchen.

Three days later he's once again sitting in his chair reading and she repeats the frying-pan attack.

Bloke: 'What the hell was that for this time?'

Wife: 'Your horse phoned.'

Three blokes are out fishing, when out of the blue they catch a mermaid. She begs to be set free and offers to grant each of them a wish to let her go. One of the blokes doesn't believe it, and says: 'OK, if you can really grant wishes, double my IQ.' The mermaid says: 'Done.' Suddenly, the bloke starts reciting Shakespeare flawlessly and analysing it with extreme insight.

The second bloke is so amazed, he says to the mermaid: 'Triple my IQ.' The mermaid says: 'Done.' And the bloke starts to spout out the mathematical solutions to problems that have been stumping the world's greatest mathematicians.

The last bloke is so enthralled with the changes in his friends that he says to the mermaid: 'Quintuple my IQ.' The mermaid looks at him and says: 'I normally don't try to change people's minds when they make a wish, but I really wish you'd reconsider.'

The bloke says: 'No, I want you to increase my IQ times five, and if you don't do it, I won't set you free.'

'Please,' says the mermaid. 'You don't know what you're asking … it'll change your entire view on the universe. Ask for something else … a million dollars, anything?' But no matter what the mermaid said, the bloke insisted on having his IQ increased by five times its usual power.

So the mermaid sighs and says: 'Done.'

And he becomes a woman …

A bloke walks into the bedroom to find his wife jumping up and down on the bed. She says: 'I've just had my annual check-up and the doctor says I may be 45, but I've got the breasts of an 18 year old!'

'Yeah,' says the bloke. 'And what did he say about your 45-year-old arse?'

'Oh, he didn't mention you, dear.'

An **obnoxious bloke** tries to **apologise** to a **female** colleague, saying: 'I'm **sorry** I put you in such an **awkward position** the other day.' Not feeling in a **forgiving mood,** she replies:

'There's not a position between one and 69 that I'd ever care to be in with you.'

A bloke and a woman are involved in a terrible car accident. Both of their cars are totally demolished, but amazingly, neither of them is hurt. After they crawl out of their cars, the woman says: 'So, you're a man? That's interesting. I'm a woman. Wow, just look at our cars! There's nothing left, but fortunately, we're unhurt. This must be a sign from God that we should meet and be friends, and live together in peace for the rest of our days.' Flattered, the man replied: 'Oh yes, I agree with you completely! This must be a sign from God!'

The woman continued: 'And look at this, here's another miracle: my car is completely demolished but this bottle of wine didn't break. Surely God wants us to drink this wine and celebrate our good fortune.' Then she hands the bottle to the man. The man nods his head in agreement, opens the bottle and drinks half of it and then hands it back to the woman. The woman takes the bottle, immediately puts the cap back on and hands it back to the man. The man asks: 'Aren't you having any?' The woman replies: 'No, I think I'll wait for the police.'

A newly-wed couple are just beginning their honeymoon. The bloke takes off his trousers, gives them to the girl and tells her to put them on. They're four sizes too big, so she says: 'There's no way I can wear these.'

'Good,' he replies. 'Now you know who wears the trousers in this relationship.'

Then she takes her tiny knickers off and says: 'OK, put these on.'

'I can't get into them,' the bloke says.

And she replies: 'Correct, unless you change your attitude.'